THE CHARLES ELIOT NORTON LECTURES, 1977–1978

THE GENESIS
OF SECRECY

THE GENESIS OF SECRECY

On the Interpretation of Narrative

FRANK KERMODE

HARVARD UNIVERSITY PRESS
CAMBRIDGE, MASSACHUSETTS
LONDON, ENGLAND
1979

Library of Congress Cataloging in Publication Data

Kermode, John Frank.
The genesis of secrecy.

(The Charles Eliot Norton lectures; 1977–1978)
Includes bibliographical references and index.
1. Hermeneutics. 2. Narration (Rhetoric) I. Title.
II. Series.
PN81.K4   801'.95   78–23403
ISBN 0–674–34525–8

Robert Frost's "Directive" is quoted by permission
of Holt Rinehart and Winston from The Poetry of
Robert Frost, edited by Edward Connery Lathem
(copyright 1947, © 1969 by Holt, Rinehart and
Winston, © 1975 by Lesley Frost Ballantine)

To Those Outside

ἐκείνοις δὲ τοῖς ἔξω ἐν παραβολαῖς τὰ πάντα γίνεται·

Preface

A PERSON of my profession can hardly imagine a greater compliment, or a richer source of pleasure, than an invitation to deliver the Charles Eliot Norton lectures. He will have one of the best audiences in the world: the gifted young, wonderfully receptive, quite unafraid of one's subject, however new to them; their learned elders, equally generous, equally undeterred by blizzard or disagreement. It is hardly to be hoped, however, that he will find his pleasure untainted by anxiety. The receipt of such an invitation does not of itself make him a more learned and stimulating man. He remains as he is, though he will respond by trying to make whatever it may be that is at the moment interesting to him a matter of interest to others. Over the past few years I had found myself increasingly concerned with problems of interpretation — problems of practice and also of theory — especially as they presented themselves in narrative, but also, because narrative seems so central, in many other areas. It was this preoccupation that stimulated my interest in biblical exegesis and hermeneutics.

The history of the rules and theory of interpretation — of hermeneutics as it used to be, before philosophy appropriated it — is closely linked with that of biblical exegesis; the exegetes drew up the rules or canons, refined them, distinguished between different kinds of hermeneutic activity, and expanded the whole subject to include such questions as what makes interpretation possible, how its process is affected by the lapse of time between the writing and the interpreting, what may be controlled by prescriptive rules of conduct, and what must be left to the divinatory genius of the interpreter. Until quite recently secular scholars in America and England paid very little attention to the subject, and all the major developments were of German origin. Nor has secular literary criticism shown much interest in biblical criticism, except when it has seemed essential to research of the more antiquarian kinds.

I think this is unfortunate, for several reasons. First, the scholarly quality and discipline of the best biblical study is high enough to be, in many ways, exemplary to us. Secondly, institutional forces, both enabling and constraining, are much more visibly at work in the biblical forms of interpretation. All interpretative activity is subject to cultural predispositions and institutional caveats; the best students are now both more knowledgeable and more suspicious than they used to be, but the constraints continue to exist. We cannot emigrate from our historical moment, nor from a society that depends on institutions for continuity as well as for the provision of occasions for dissent, successful or not, on the part of the deviant or the charismatic. The ecclesiastical institution has general control over biblical exegesis, though it is not uniformly powerful, and does not rule out bold speculations; historically, indeed, it has not inhibited work that it has had no choice but to condemn. But for the most part the practitioners have had some prior commitment to Christianity, some "doctrinal adhesion" (to borrow I. A. Richards' expression), which is a distinguishing mark since secular critics as a rule do not have one, unless it is that doctrinal adhesions are bad things. Few would undertake the ardors of the training held necessary for serious work in biblical criticism without some such prior commitment; it follows that there is a family resemblance between the most disparate works in the field, and a visible difference of interest and manner from almost all secular criticism.

Of late, however, biblical critics have been looking over the fence and noting the methods and achievements of the secular arm; sacred and profane texts are more than ever before discussed in the same book or article. For a secular critic to work on the reserved sacred texts, as I have chosen to do, is rarer. It is easy to understand why this should be so: there is a lack of interest (which I deplore but recognize); and there is a lack of necessary skills. The volume of scholarship is dismaying, and any outsider is bound to make mistakes. I am sure I have done so, in the teeth of good advice. The linguistic requirement is formidable, and I myself had better say at once that I have no Aramaic or Hebrew, only enough Greek, and German so enfeebled that whenever possible I use translations. I have undertaken the studies here reported only because the importance of the subject, and the need of a secular approach, justify a measure of rashness. I think the gospels need to be talked about by critics of a quite unecclesiastical formation.

The six chapters that follow are somewhat expanded versions of six lectures in which problems of interpretation are considered suggestively, not systematically. That the gospels offer peculiar opportunities to anybody making inquiries of this sort seems obvious; indeed I can think of no other texts so promising. I included in the original draft of the lectures a rather long discussion of the relationship between the four texts; for that relationship, very complex, sometimes close and sometimes not, constitutes a great portion of the boon. But I came to see that such a discussion, which would in any case have lacked the extraordinary subtlety and intimacy of detail characteristic of professional argument on this head, could only make the wrong kind of claim on a general audience. I asked them instead to accept a rather simple (but I think essentially correct) view of the matter: a downright assertion that Mark came first, that Matthew and Luke made substantial use of Mark, and that John, in a different tradition, was relatively, though not entirely, on his own. Mark, who presents extremely difficult and interesting problems of interpretation, is my central text; but I have been concerned less with offering an interpretation of Mark than with indicating possibilities of interpretation which are not those of the professionals, or not exploited in the same ways, though I have drawn very freely on their work.

Acts of interpretation are required at every stage in the life of a narrative; its earliest form must itself be an interpretation of some precedent fable. (I use this term in a somewhat specialized sense, to be explained in Chapter Four.) Mark is already an interpretation; Matthew and Luke are in large part interpretations of Mark. There comes a point where interpretation by the invention of new narrative is halted; in the present instance that point was reached with the establishment of a canon of four gospels. Interpretation thereafter usually continues in commentary. These interpretative continuities are illuminated, I have suggested, by the practice of midrash. By midrash the interpreter, either by rewriting the story or explaining it in a more acceptable sense, bridges the gap between an original and a modern audience. The word derives from *dārash*, to probe or examine; however the work is done, whether by fictive augmentation and change or by commentary, its object is to penetrate the surface and reveal a secret sense; to show what is concealed in what is proclaimed.

It would be wrong, I think, to suppose that this kind of interpretation is specific to sacred texts. Secular authors also interpret their own fables. The process is abundantly documented by Henry James in his Notebooks and Prefaces. There is some *donnée*, some small seed of talk: "a child . . . was *divided* by its parents in consequence of their being divorced. The court, for some reason, didn't, as it might have done, give the child exclusively to either parent, but decreed that it was to spend its time equally with each — that is, alternately." Long entries over the next four years provide a picture of James excitedly probing, examining, altering — killing off the divorced parents and resuscitating them. "Voyons, voyons," he exhorts himself; and "the interminable little Maisie" grows from a projected "incident" of 5000 words into the long novel *What Maisie Knew*, the final form of which differs even from the very full final scenario. Then the work is handed over to the commentators, the most important of whom is James himself, in the Preface added for the New York edition. At this stage interpretation suffers under the restriction that the commentator may not rewrite or interpolate new narrative and interfere with "the march of an action"; but the degree of freedom left to him is still great, and no one will suppose that James's own afterword exhausts the possibilities of interpretation. There are senses concealed from the original as from all other diviners.

The gospels have a particular value to a student of these processes, for they were written by men who worked in a long tradition of midrash. Large parts of the Old Testament owe their form to the practice, and it has even been said that the Torah itself is midrash: narrative interpretation of a narrative, a way of finding in an existing narrative the potential of more narrative. I have tried to use the gospels as prime examples of interpretation in narrative. I have also tried to use them as instances of certain problems common to the interpretation of all texts, such as the elusiveness of secret senses, their way of varying from one period and one person to another; their status with respect to what a cultural or institutional consensus chooses to regard as well-formed narrative; their relation, as narratives purporting to be historical reports, to fact.

This book consists, then, of a number of approaches to general problems of interpretation. They seem to be problems of importance, for, broadly conceived, the power to make interpretations is an indispensable instrument of survival in the world, and it works there as it works on literary texts. In all the works of interpretation there are insiders and outsiders, the former having, or professing to have, immediate access to the mystery, the latter randomly scattered across space and time, and excluded from the elect who mistrust or despise their unauthorized divinations, which may indeed, for all the delight they give, be without absolute value. The world, to the outsider, is obscurely organized and it is a blessing, though possibly a delusive one, that the world is also, to use Whitehead's expression, "patient of interpretation in terms of whatever happens to interest us." What always interests us is the sense concealed in the proclamation. If we cannot agree about the nature of the secret, we are nevertheless compelled to agree that secrecy exists, the source of the interpreter's pleasures, but also of his necessary disappointment.

QUOTATIONS from the Bible are often from the Revised Standard Version, but I have departed from it whenever I saw reason to do so; it hardly seemed necessary to explain such departures.

Contents

I have kept hidden at the instep arch
Of an old cedar at the waterside
A broken drinking goblet like the Grail
Under a spell so the wrong ones can't find it,
So can't get saved, as Saint Mark says they mustn't.

Robert Frost

I

Carnal
and
Spiritual Senses

*The natural man receives not
the things of the spirit . . .
for they are foolishness to him.*
1 Corinthians 2:14

THE GOD HERMES is the patron of thieves, merchants, and travelers; of heralds and what heralds pronounce, their *kērygma.* He also has to do with oracles, including a dubious sort known as *klēdōn,* which at the moment of its announcement may seem trivial or irrelevant, the secret sense declaring itself only after long delay, and in circumstances not originally foreseeable. Hermes is cunning, and occasionally violent: a trickster, a robber. So it is not surprising that he is also the patron of interpreters. Sometimes they proclaim an evident sense, like a herald; but they also use cunning, and may claim the right to be violent, and glory in it. The rules of their art, and its philosophy, are called "hermeneutics." This word itself, after centuries of innocent use, turns out to have secret senses; for it is now thought by some to connote the most serious philosophical inquiry, to be the means whereby they effect a necessary subversion of the old metaphysics. Even in its more restricted application, which is related to the interpretation of texts, the word covers a considerable range of activity, from the plain proclamation of sense to oracular intimations of which the true understanding may be delayed for generations, emerging in historical circumstances quite unlike those in which the oracle spoke. Such operations may require the professional exercise of stealth or violence.

Interpreters usually belong to an institution, such a guild as heralds, toastmasters, thieves, and merchants have been known to form; and as members they enjoy certain privileges and suffer certain constraints. Perhaps the most important of these are the right to affirm, and the obligation to accept, the superiority of latent over manifest sense. It is a preference of great antiquity, though we recognize it as modern when we see it in its Freudian form. Of the psychoanalytical institution, as of all institutions of interpretation, Hermes is patron. He is the god of going-between: between the dead and the living, but also between the latent and the manifest (god, one might say, of the third ear), and between the text, whether plain or hermetic, and the dying generations of its readers.

This book is about interpretation, an interpretation of interpretation, and I hope the invocation to Hermes will therefore seem appropriate. But in our tradition the arts and the philosophy of interpretation have been developed to a very great extent by men who studied a special kerygma, and owed allegiance to a different god. He handed down not only a text for them to interpret, but also rules and a theory of interpretation. The theory seems, however daunting, plain enough, though like many clear things it darkens under the interpreter's gaze. Here, at the outset, we need to confront it in its original, uncompromising, and disquieting form.

When Jesus was asked to explain the purpose of his parables, he described them as stories *told to them without* — to outsiders — with the express purpose of concealing a mystery that was to be understood only by insiders. So Mark tells us: speaking to the Twelve, Jesus said, "To you has been given the secret of the kingdom of God, but for those outside everything is in parables; so that they may indeed see but not perceive, and may indeed hear but not understand; lest they should turn again, and be forgiven" (4:11–12).

I have given the translation of the Revised Standard Version, which might be varied — perhaps "parables" should be "riddles" — but unless certain words here mean what they do not usually mean the sense of Jesus' saying is plain enough. Only the insiders can have access to the true sense of these stories.

"For to him who has will more be given; and from him who has not, even what he has will be taken away." To divine the true, the latent sense, you need to be of the elect, of the institution. Outsiders must content themselves with the manifest, and pay a supreme penalty for doing so. Only those who already know the mysteries — what the stories really mean — can discover what the stories really mean. As a matter of fact, the teacher, on the very occasion when he pronounced this rule, showed himself irritated with his elect for seeking explanations of what they already, in principle, knew. And, if we are to believe Mark, they continued to be slow learners, prone to absurd error. But they did know that even plain stories mean more than they seem to say, that they may contain mysteries inaccessible to all but privileged interpreters — and perhaps not always with any great measure of certainty even to them.

As I shall try to explain in the second chapter, the true sense of this theory of parable interpretation is much disputed; cunning ways are found of making it mean other than it seems to say, involving accusations of treachery in redactors and scribes, and even in the Greek language as Mark used it. But in my opinion the distinction holds, that in this tradition insiders can hope to achieve correct interpretations, though their hope may be frequently, perhaps always, disappointed; whereas those outside cannot. There is seeing and hearing, which are what naive listeners and readers do; and there is perceiving and understanding, which are in principle reserved to an elect. The apocryphal Epistle to Barnabas distinguishes between those within and those without by saying that the former have circumcised ears and the latter not. And all who teach and practice interpretation, whichever god is their patron, are in the business of aural circumcision. We have to see that another generation of elect interpreters will be ready to succeed us.

More interpreters mean more interpretations. We may seek (and usually we achieve) a measure of institutional control over the speed and character of the changes, but we rightly assume they will occur, for they have done so throughout the existence of every text that commands institutional approval and continuous interpretative attention. There is a perpetual *aggiorna-*

mento of the latent senses. Such change may be in some degree willed; there are alterations of mode caused by the need to make one's seniors seem obsolete, or by political or commercial pressures, or simply by the charisma of some heresiarch. There are even accessions to what might be broadly termed philological knowledge, such as the Dead Sea Scrolls or the Gnostic library of Nag Hamadi, though these discoveries are really too great for my present occasion; it would be enough to cite some item of information bearing on the available senses of a particular word in the Greek of Mark or the English of Chaucer. But these obvious agencies do not explain interpretative change. Our acts of divination — for the acts that determine undetected latent sense are properly so called — our divinations are made necessary by the fact of our occupying, inescapably, a position in history which is not the position of the text we cultivate, and not a position of which we have much objective understanding, though it helps to constitute the complex of prejudices we bring to the task of discovering a sense, for us, in the text we value (another element of prejudice). The character of our encounter with ancient texts is accordingly highly problematical, though in that respect it differs only in degree from that of our encounter with any text. These are some of the considerations that preoccupy philosophers of interpretation, and whoever forsakes the manifest, carnal sense of the outsider and deals with the latent or spiritual must in some measure embroil himself in the problems of that philosophy — which is itself subject to unknowable historical limitation, and subject to change.

It is of course true that individual acts of interpretation are rarely if ever performed in full consciousness of these meta-interpretative considerations. And although we are aware how much any interpretation must depend on a tacit form of knowing acquired from institutional training, we tend to reserve our highest praise for those interpretations that seem most intuitive, most theory-free, seeming to proceed from some untrammeled divinatory impulse, having the gratuity, the fortuity of genius. The possibility of such divinations may explain why Hermes once laid claim to a share in the lyre of Apollo. We admire their natural violence or cunning, or their lyric force, and only later do we reason about them, and see how, in spite of everything, the institution helped to shape them. The best psychoanalysts are admired by their colleagues not for their theoretical mastery or correctness, but for their powers of divination, for the acuteness of their third ear. That these powers were partly created by, remain under the control of, and derive their high value from, the historical institution of psychoanalysis is a truth that emerges in subsequent discussion. So it is with the interpretation of written texts. The discovery of latent senses may appear to be a spontaneous, individual achievement; but it is privileged and constrained by the community of the ear, whether tertiary or circumcised.

Here is an example of the way latent sense is detected. The text is Henry Green's novel *Party Going*.[1] It is not yet part of the secular canon; that is, it has not been guaranteed to be of such value that every effort of exegesis is justified without argument, as it is in the cases of, say, Joyce and Faulkner. A confession that one had not read *Party Going* would not be humiliating (a rule-of-thumb of canonicity). In the circumstances I had better give a brief account of it. Probably, in doing so, I shall unconsciously cheat a bit, and favor the particular interpretation that follows. I cannot make sense of a part without placing it in relation to a whole: that is common sense, and also a basic principle of interpretation-theory. And do not suppose that the conformity of such principles with common sense is always so obvious. Theory can obscure as well as facilitate. It amused Nietzsche to remind us that the name of Schleiermacher, one of the founding fathers of modern hermeneutics, means "veil-maker." However, the fact is that without some fore-understanding of the whole we can make no sense of the part; and our fore-understanding of the whole is largely constructed from our present understanding of the part. The summary I shall now offer is a substitute for a fore-understanding of the whole, no doubt, as I say, subject to that benign distortion which usually or always accompanies interpretation, a civilized form of the old violence and stealth.

Why do I make these preliminaries so cautious, when all I

intend is to tell a story? Because I hope that this display of hermeneutic scrupulosity will make things easier for me later. There are metacritical moves available to frustrate almost any of the operations I want to conduct, and it would be very tedious always to be trying to forestall them. Allow me, then, to say that *Party Going* is recognizably what is known as a novel, and that it has a followable narrative, of which it is possible to give a conventional, though of course partial, account.

A party of rich young persons congregates at a London railway station, at some date, we may suppose, in the Thirties. They are off on a winter holiday in the south, we may suppose, of France. Fog prevents the departure of their train. The station, which is in the City of London, is a commuter station as well as a continental terminal, and as the City offices close the concourse is jammed by thousands of commuters unable to get home. The father of one of the rich girls is a director of the railway company, and enjoins the stationmaster to see to the comfort of the holiday party. He accommodates them in the station hotel, where they pass the time in petty jealousies, arid sexual banter, gossip, drinking, taking baths, and complaining about the service. From their windows they can look down on the thousands in the foggy concourse; among them, they hope, are their own servants, guarding the luggage. Beyond stretch the deserted departure platforms. As the crowds increase the hotel is sealed off by steel doors. The party, we are told, cannot get out, and the commuters cannot get in. Police arrive in strength to control the crowds, but they remain good-humored.

One man of the party is concerned about the fate of the luggage. He accosts a mysterious stranger, who has been hanging about inside the hotel, and bribes him to get out into the concourse and check that the luggage is safe. This stranger does get out, and does find the servants, but he exceeds his brief by trying to take the luggage away, which the servants will not allow him to do. Meanwhile the party within is augmented first by the arrival of a pampered beauty named Amabel, and then, at the very end, by that of Embassy Richard, a young man whose escapades have formed a considerable part of their gossip.

By the time he arrives the fog has lifted and the trains can run again.

My account of Green's novel, however defective, may at least serve to suggest that it belongs to a class of narratives which *have* to mean more, or other, than they manifestly say. How do we know this? First because we know that many insiders think well of Henry Green, so we assume that the book is not trivial and vacuous, even if it seems so at first. This prejudice is supported by many signs that the writing, however odd, is not incompetent. Yet the formal anagnorisis or recognition of Embassy Richard is a wantonly empty gesture, and the characters are mindless; does this mean simply that they *are* disgustingly trivial, vacuously privileged, and shown at tedious length to be so? The uncircumcised ear is disappointed; this author is not a best-seller. But the initiate assumes that the absence of some usual satisfactions, the disappointment of conventional expectations, connote the existence of other satisfactions, deeper and more difficult, inaccessible to those who see without perceiving and hear without understanding.

By what divinatory method are they to be reached? The process may well involve putting a lot of exegetical pressure on one point. How about that mysterious stranger, the one who escaped from the hotel to see if the baggage was safe? As a matter of fact, we first met him very early in the book, in these circumstances. Miss Fellowes, the aunt of one of the rich girls, is in the station for no other reason than to see her niece off. Miss Fellowes is old — fifty-one, in fact. On the first page of the book a pigeon falls out of the fog and lies dead at her feet. Attended by a chorus of two nannies who, although they know her well, do not greet her, she carries the bird into the ladies' lavatory and carefully washes it. Then she wraps it in brown paper and, carrying her parcel, enters a station bar and orders whiskey. She appears to be unwell, and this is observed not only by the nannies but by a certain "rough-looking customer." An emissary from the young people's party happens upon Miss Fellowes in the bar. The hotel is still open, and she is taken to it. The nannies and the rough-looking customer follow her in.

This fellow has a curious way of speaking, using several different working-class accents, but sometimes deviating without warning into the authoritative tones of upper-class English. His manners fluctuate in the same way. When a hotel doctor, who may think Miss Fellowes has merely been drinking, affirms that she has nothing wrong with her that a rest will not put right, the rough-looking customer dissents. He is confident that she is very sick indeed. Thus he attracts some attention to himself; but nobody knows who he is. The oddities of his behavior are vaguely explained by the supposition that he is a hotel detective. Anyway, he accepts a commission to inspect the luggage, and, not without difficulty, gets out of the firmly shuttered hotel.

Hermes, as patron of travelers, may preside over any railway station; as god of boundaries and messenger between worlds he may defy the steel doors of this hotel. As thief he might eye the luggage of the very rich. Even in Homer he retains some of the marks of his proletarian origins, and is represented both as an archaic rustic and an upper-class ephebe, so it is not surprising that he might violate or confuse the once infallible code of English class accents. Homer's word for such persons as this stranger is "hired boundary-crosser." [2] But not only merchants, travelers, heralds, and thieves cross boundaries; so do the dying. And our stranger is associated not only with Miss Fellowes, who may be dying, but with the choric nannies, nannies being poor people who cross the thresholds of rich houses in order to attend, with appropriate forms of deference, to the needs of the recently born and sometimes to those of the dying — the text reminds us of their expertness in the very early diagnosis of terminal illnesses. So, in their way, they are close enough to Hermes, who as psychopomp conducts the dead to the underworld. Our stranger moves into and out of death's dream kingdom, this concourse, this place of departures. It is often enough, indeed ostentatiously, compared to a graveyard, though it is a real station in the unreal City of London, full of commuters, brothers and sisters of that crowd that flows over London Bridge at nine and back at five-thirty: I had not thought death had undone so many.

The drop from the lowest hotel window into the concourse is measured thus: a man standing on another's man's shoulders can just kiss a maid leaning out. Of what may this be a figure? And why, when among the rich in the hotel there is only a prurient, timid, low-toned sexuality, do we find among the proletarians in the concourse a capacity for sexual joy? The servant Thompson, guarding the luggage, is beautifully and gratuitously kissed by a girl called Emily, whom he has never seen before; bewildered by pleasure, he remarks that she "came up out of the bloody ground" to do it. Are we here under the rule of some phallic caduceus, on a boundary marked by some phallic herm? Whatever may be said about that, one thing is sure: as interpreters we are beginning to move more freely, and to invite esoteric dispute.

Once free of the constraints of the simple primary sense, we begin to seize on those more interesting — let us say spiritual — senses that failed to manifest themselves in the course of a, let us say, carnal reading. Carnal readings are much the same. Spiritual readings are all different. Speculation thrives; we each want to say something different about the same text. Nor is there a foreseeable end to the things that might be said; one divination breeds another. Think of all those references to the lustrated and parceled pigeon — for the bird is always coming back, though in my first, my carnal, account of the book it was not mentioned at all, as if it were a mere arabesque, of no substantive interest. It is consigned to a trashbin, recovered, spoken of not only by Miss Fellowes and those young people who saw her with her parcel, but also by other characters who, so far as we are informed, have had no opportunity to learn of the opening incident. Once loose in the text, the pigeon seems to alight at random on anything. Now interpretation abhors the random, which is one reason why, in the most modern school of criticism, it has become a dirty word, a term of censure. Interpretation will seek relations between the cleansing of the bird and the long, narcissistic, teasing, ritual bath of beautiful Amabel. It will find, in some secondary world of magic and ritual, an explanation for the lucky, apotropaic toys carried everywhere by silly Julia. It may go on to provide this fiction with a mythological structure, a satisfying spiritual order, instead of the trivial carnal order of the primary narrative. Should we go on to say, in a manner now modish, that the text, in the end, interprets itself or enacts its own interpretation? This is the latest of Hermes' tricks, when the interpretation vanishes into the text, or the text into the interpretation.

Some more level-headed thinkers might at this point ask what sounds like a very pertinent question. If all this is "in" the book, why hasn't it been noticed before? Weren't good early readers as well or even better equipped to see what was going on? Did they relate it to an occult mythological center? I am not aware that they did. The literary historian can tell us that at the time of the book's writing ("London, 1931–8" is inscribed at its end) there was a fashionable doctrine that myth could give shape and meaning to contemporary experience, that vast panorama of futility. And during these years good readers were reading *Ulysses,* which prompted that doctrine, and *The Waste Land,* the work of its originator. They were also reading Freud, who sought interpretations at just such junctures of the occult and the representable, in condensations and displacements that disturb the surface of the verisimilar and the well formed — in a manner not wholly unlike what might be supposed of this story which, set in a foggy London station, is seen, under the lamp of interpretation, to have occulted its true sense.

Yet so far as I know nobody did say anything of this sort. Nevertheless, we do not regard this as evidence that we are on the wrong track. We all assume that good readings may very well be made, perhaps for the first time, long after the death of the author and his contemporaries. They will, of course, be spiritual not carnal readings, insiders' readings. Once the institution licenses a text for full-scale exegetical exploitation there is no limit. Our divinatory powers grow as the primary reading, carnal, manifest — the one most obvious to the first readers — loses its compelling force, its obviousness.

Party Going belongs, historically, to the years of the Depression, and the threat of war. Its readers were doubtless preoccupied by the increasing grossness of the contrasts between rich and poor. The imminence of revolution was often proclaimed, and war, likely to launch so great a crowd across the final boundary, was thought certain. Henry Green was known to be a rich man who had worked on the floor of his own factory; he was an Old Etonian and a Communist sympathizer. His previous novel, *Living*, had been praised for the unmatched accuracy and sympathy of its rendering of working-class speech and behavior. Less note was taken of the fact that it swarmed mysteriously with pigeons; that it contained invitations to interpretative license, many extraordinary rhetorical figurations, many narrative and stylistic eccentricities. Since they made no obvious contribution to the primary sense, these eccentricities were not, as people now say, "foregrounded" in interpretation. They stayed in the mind, I think, mostly as a sort of mnemonic flavor, distinguishing this from true proletarian fiction. In much the same way it would have been easy to read *Party Going* simply, as an expression of disgust at the conduct of the immature, ostentatious rich, with their insipid sexuality and carelessly cruel manners, and of admiration, even tenderness, for the poor — humble people who expect very little, and are patient, cheerful, competent.

Nor need such a reading be as naive as I suggested. The rich, for obvious reasons, prefer social simplicity. On the one hand there are nannies and other old-fashioned servants, including chauffeurs, all of whom know how to behave because they are bound to the service of masters. On the other there are unliveried members of the lower class, taxi-drivers, for instance, whom one insults, and who may be insolent if one walks away without paying the fare. They are disagreeable, but one knows them. What is upsetting is the class of person who cannot be so easily placed, like the messenger who may be a hotel detective or even a doctor, yet accepts ten shillings to execute an errand. It is the presence on the scene of such socially uncertain persons that makes one hesitate between two views of the masses: are they a foul many-headed beast, with designs on one's daughters and one's property, or are they in truth reassuringly docile under what, if one thinks about it, one must admit to be provoking circumstances? "Dear good English people, who never make trouble no matter how bad it is, come what may no matter." So says silly Julia, though whether she is silly in saying this we cannot tell, and anyway she is only imitating the way her elders have been cheering themselves up. In short, we are being told about the peculiar bad faith of the upper classes in the period just before World War II.

This kind of reading, originating within the horizon of a particular period, cannot be disallowed; but it cannot, either, disqualify others which do not so originate, are differently focused, yet can be established as legitimate and interesting (which is practically the same thing as "institutionally acceptable"). Any one such focus is, of course, chosen at the expense of others, and is bound to ignore much of the information offered by the text; extreme instances of this always necessary neglect are the Freudian and Lévi-Straussian types of analysis. The mythological reading I proposed is not only blind and deaf to the political reading; it also ignores the whole linguistic and rhetorical dimension of the novel. For example: where normal English usage calls for definite articles, *Party Going* often uses demonstratives ("those two nannies," "that bird"). This can be very unsettling, like the wholesale omission of articles in *Living*; it is a kind of grammatical assertion of the uniqueness of the text, a hint, perhaps, that it is not easily reducible to something else. Thus does a stylistic eccentricity hamper the interpreter, one of whose most useful moves is to see his text in relation to some larger whole: an oeuvre, a genre, some organized corpus like mythology.

In the end some such move must be made; but these hints of irreducibility can have a severely qualifying effect on interpretative strategies like the one I used when I placed the Hermes figure in the very center of *Party Going*. In Green's *Loving*, for instance, there is great play with conventional narrative expectations, and there are mythological suggestions and configurations that announce themselves far more positively than Hermes did; but they usually flash and fade at once, as if the point were only to hint that there *might* be a point when there *can't* be one if you allow the book to be what it really is. *Loving* seems also to be concerned with class, even, a little, with the war that threatened in *Party Going*; but indications of such an interest are repeatedly submerged in great washes of color, or effaced by doodles of sensual delight, as when the lovely house-maids caress each other, or dance in the great ballroom, or are converted — by the play of light, or by doves and peacocks clustering on them or strutting before them — into poetry. In such writing there is created an expectation of much beautiful willfulness, and the reader must sometimes recognize it. He may thus be made to understand that his expectation of a re-ward for bringing the surprising into conformity with the usual is no more justified than any other bourgeois expectation of docile service, or of licit requirements assiduously satisfied. Thus do texts interpret, or deceive, their interpreters, who should know they do so, and make allowances for it.

Henry Green, as it happens, gave his views on some of these matters. He said that the laws of the text declare themselves only in the course of its writing, so that no conformity with ex-ternal models should be expected. Now Green — or Yorke, for that was his real name, and we are getting personal — Yorke happened to be a bit deaf; and he greatly valued the obliquities this disability conferred upon conversation. In a *Paris Review* interview he offered his deafness as an explanation of the "nonrepresentational" character of his books. "For instance, the very deaf, as I am, hear the most astounding things all round them, which have not, in fact, been said. This enlivens my replies until, through mishearing, a new level of communi-cation is reached." In the course of the interview there is a curious example of the generation of a new theme by mishear-ing. At one point Green suddenly remarks that "*Suttee* . . . is the suicide — now forbidden — of a Hindu wife on her hus-band's flaming bier." He goes on to say that he does not wish his own wife to do this when his time comes; "and with great respect, as I know her, she won't." What the interviewer had said to provoke this excursion was that some people regarded Green's novels as too *subtle*. He explained this. "Oh, *subtle*," says Green. "How dull!" [3]

A good many things sit in Green's novels the way this dis-quisition on Hindu funeral customs sits in the interview. There's a sort of intermittency, a willful narrative deafness, a preference for the interesting over the obvious and sequential. From *suttee* there flowers an apparently irrelevant but interesting squiggle; *subtle* commands only a dully civil response. So, amid all the plausible talk, there occur in these books pigeons and doves, peacocks and roses. Green was always interested in the narrative effect of sensory failure. His first, undergraduate, novel, *Blindness,* has a hero who must reconfront the world after losing his sight in an accident. In *Loving* there is a marvelous game of blindman's buff, an emblem, perhaps, of his own games. Sensory failure, an interruption in the conventional processing of information, in our knowing dully, for the sake of convenience, where and what we are, may make for a momentary strangeness in the world or in the book. The effect may be very grand, though it can be explained as dependent on the same method as a simple joke, such as that which tells of two deaf men driving along in a car: "This is Wembley." "No, it's Thursday." "So am I, let's stop and have a drink." Green liked to exploit what may through a simple figure be thought of as the sensory limitations to which narrative is prone: blindness, deafness, an intermittency of memory — as in the discourse of the senile there may recur trivial images of infancy, acquiring what inexplicable import they have simply by the fact of recurrence and repetition; or, on the other hand, long passages of life may be annihilated by mere forgetfulness. Modern critical theory occasionally remembers to mention forgetfulness; to put it at its lowest, it is a great aid to interpretation, whether the writer's or the reader's. A text with all its wits about it would see and hear and remember too much, would always say "subtlety" plainly and audibly; a reader with all his dull wits about him would never hear "suttee." There would be no game, only a carnal world and not the blindman's buff of the spirit. The expected would never be finessed for the sake of those two lovely girls who danced in every droplet of an immense chandelier. To be blessedly fallible, to have the capacity to subvert manifest senses, is the mark of good enough readers and good enough texts.

Yet all narratives are capable of darkness; the oracular is always there or thereabouts, accessible if only by a sensory failure; and much writing we think of as peculiarly modern is in part a rediscovery of the oracular, and sometimes an exploitation of sensory failure. One motive of this modernism was the desire to break with a tradition of writing supposed to have been based on a mistaken or dishonest desire to eliminate the oracular by simple plausibility in the registration of a real world, and by connivance with vulgar notions of cause and closure — to make false sense by means of a false realism. We should not forget (reminding ourselves that forgetfulness is also an important factor in the history of criticism) that narratives of this kind — intermittent, forgetful, at times blind or deaf — existed long ago; their varying focus, fractured surfaces, overdeterminations, displacements, have constituted a perpetual invitation to all inquirers after latent sense, a perpetual challenge to those more sober interpreters who want to know how they came to be as they, very idiosyncratically, are. The gospels ought to be the prize song of exegetical apprentices.

Thus far I have been exercising myself on familiar material, and without much risk; but I come now to the performance I have undertaken, which is to speak mainly of the gospel narratives, especially Mark. This, I had best be plain, I shall do in a wholly secular way. There is a doctrine which holds that it is wrong to make division between sacred and secular hermeneutics; the doctrine is two hundred years old at least, and seems to pass as conventional wisdom. Yet it is common enough for the professionals, the exegetes de métier, to maintain that a correct understanding of the New Testament may be had only by the faithful; the outsiders will see without perceiving, hear without understanding. I suppose the positions can be reconciled, but that is not my business. Ecclesiastical institutions are, like others, understandably anxious to protect themselves against impious intruders. Such persons are in any case unlikely to know enough in a merely technical sense, spiritual illumination apart. Yet they are, though secular, the heirs of the exegetical and hermeneutic traditions. Scrupulosity of method, subtlety of understanding and explication, the general philosophy of interpretation as it developed in the New Testament tradition, may seem to them part of their just birthright.

They should be allowed their secular say on the cardinal texts.

At this point it may be useful to state in summary fashion some of the rules and cautions I hope to have elicited from my exercise on *Party Going*, for they ought to be remembered when we approach this rather different set of narratives. First, we need some assurance that a book has sufficient value — and what is aught but as 'tis valued? — to warrant the kind of attention we are proposing to give it. A mercantile approach; but Hermes is patron of merchants. More formally, this high valuation is achieved by including the text in a canon, as for example with Mark.

Secondly, there is the matter of the circumcised ear. It is true that outsiders also interpret; the most naive reading of a text, that treats it, for example, as a transparent account of reality, and picks up only the clues that enable it to satisfy the most conventional expectations, say of coherence and closure, is an interpretation. A reading at the next level, which is as spiritual to carnal, perceiving to seeing, understanding to hearing, calls for divination: violence or cunning, the patronage of the psychopomp.

Thirdly, there is the *moment* of interpretation, the discovery or choice of what, after Dilthey, might be called an "impression-point." [4] One may perceive in a life some moment that gives sense and structure to the whole, and it need not come at the end of the life; Dilthey cites the conversion of Augustine, which made sense of the apparently unrelated flux of events on which it supervened — it is a part with a relation of particular privilege to the whole. A work of art, he believed, would have this same impression-point, around which the whole gestalt must be articulated. So we, with our specialized interpreter's senses, must believe; and we may even believe (though Dilthey did not say so, for his attention was at this moment focused on the work rather than the interpretation) that particular divinations may discover several or many such points. For *Party Going* I gave as example the crossing of a boundary by our Hermes, the stranger who got out of the closed hotel. Other interpreters would certainly choose different moments.

Fourthly, this divination must not be left to stand on its

own; indeed it can only be justified if we contrive to reconcile it with a larger whole. The first need is to reconcile it with the whole of the narrative in which it occurs. But we may also need to consider it in relation to a whole that is larger still: an oeuvre. We may then come upon difficulties; there may be evidence (as I suggested there was in Henry Green) that speaks against the probability of such elaborately occult figurations. (This, incidentally, is the sort of consideration often ignored by allegorizers of Shakespeare.) While we seek our intimations of latent order we may omit to notice that our text has a manifest gratuitousness, a playfulness — we might add a blindness, a deafness, a forgetfulness — that tells against our scheme. It may read *suttee* when what we seek is *subtlety*.

Fifthly, we noted that although *Party Going* had been around for forty years, nobody had come up with an interpretation of the kind I offered. But the interpretative inadequacy of our predecessors is assumed by all of us, however we explain it. We shall become accustomed to the notion that the first person to misunderstand the content of Mark was the man who wrote it; and that eighteen centuries of interpretation intervened between the first writing down of the parables and the advent of interpreters who knew how to read them. We do not usually put it as aggressively as that; we say that we recognize the historicality of the interpreter, inevitable change in modes of attention, complex interaction between present and past; we allow that our experience with the new novel alters our reading of the old, makes us more aware of the problematical character of conventions formerly assumed to be matters of nature rather than culture — and so forth. We feed our new theoretical and methodological positions into the text; they govern the course of the narrative as it appears in our interpretation, just as, in psychoanalysis, the analyst's beliefs and procedures modify the narrative of the analysand.[5] But we rarely speak as if fully aware of this complicated hermeneutical background; we are more likely to ask, am I right or wrong? And we like to be more right than anyone before us, including the author if necessary.

Lastly, there is the matter of *Party Going* being — after all — a novel. This is the problem of genre, of which I hope to say a little more in my last chapter. At present let me simply assert that the notion of a text absolutely free, absolutely open to us, in which we can "produce" meaning at will, is — as most of its proponents allow — a utopian fiction. There are constraints that shadow interpretation; and the first is genre. Of course we can say these constraints are disagreeably ideological. We can even pretend they aren't there.

All these points, in any order, I intend to raise in relation to the gospels, and especially Mark. First, though, I want to dwell for a moment on what, so far as this book is concerned, is the central problem: the existence, among initiates, of a preference for spiritual over carnal readings — that is, for interpretations that are beyond the hearing of the outsiders. If one were to write the history of such esoteric readings, and their place in our culture, one would need to make much of the moment when the Old Testament finally became joined to the New, when it was assured a permanent place in the Christian canon, from which there had been a determined attempt to exclude it. This joining, which occurred late in the second century, was of a kind that permitted Christian interpreters to assume that the more obvious senses of the Old Testament, including its historical meaning, were of small or no importance, were dangerous illusions, even. The Old Testament made sense only insofar as it prefigured Christianity. The rest of it — a great deal — was deafness, blindness, forgetfulness.

This is an extraordinary transformation. A whole literature, produced over many centuries and forming the basis of a highly developed religion and culture, is now said to have value only insofar as it complies with the fore-understanding of later interpreters. The interest of these latecomers is solely in certain arcane figurations, to which all who had supposed themselves the proper interpreters of that literature were deaf and blind. Yet this new form of interpretation, whereby, in a phrase of John Hollander's, a previously nonexistent book called the Old Testament is created out of an old one, the Torah, by a hermeneutical fiat, is a model of our own procedures, of the way we go about our higher, initiate, reading. Of course there have always been those who objected to what they saw as the dangerous destruction of history, the creation of an insatiable monster which, fed with texts, spewed forth absurd spiritual allegories.[6] But they did not prevail. And if the Old Testament could be read thus, might not the New be read in the same way?

It was, almost from the beginning. If the true sense of the Old Testament is only what is fulfilled and made plain in the New, the literal sense of the New may itself be subject to further determination. This is not merely a matter of allegory. It could be argued, for example, that as the Old signified the New Testament, so the New Testament signified the Church, which alone had power to determine its spiritual sense. For the early fifteenth-century theologian Gerson, the spiritual sense so authorized was the true literal sense; there was no appeal against the Church's judgment that could be based on the text itself. So the literal sense of the New Testament could in its turn be superseded.[7]

This supersession of senses by persons and institutions privileged to arrange it still goes on in institutions both secular and sacred. It may seem to some a game of rather limited interest, mere hermeneutic lucubration, of concern largely to monks and scholars. But it is far more than that. Without the transformation of the Old Testament I've briefly referred to, the entire history of Christianity would have been different in all respects, from the liturgical to the political. And the implication, that the New Testament might be similarly transformed, is by no means merely a monkish fantasy; it is a matter of great historical importance. It could be described as one cause of the Reformation. In a specialized form, based on the divinations of the twelfth-century Joachim da Fiore, it has had incalculable force. Joachim, interpreting scripture, prophesied the imminent arrival of the third main epoch of world history, to follow those presided over by the first and second persons of the Trinity, which corresponded to the Old and New Testaments. A third gospel — the Everlasting Gospel — would supervene, to accompany the third age or *status*, the age of the Holy Spirit. This third gospel would be quite transparent, without enigmas, without figures; for there were to be no more transformations. Time would be renewed, there would come an

emperor for the Last Days, and an angelic pope.[8] Joachim's doctrines were almost immediately exploited in the imperial propa-
ganda of Frederick II, who died in 1250. Their latest manifesta-
tion was as the *tertius status* or Third Reich of Hitler. I know
of no better example of the way in which a privileged interpretation, propounded by an elite believing that it alone has access
to the true spiritual sense of a text, may determine matters of
life and death — unless it is the horrible success of Matthew's
fiction that the Jews, after Pilate washed his hands, voluntarily
took upon themselves and their children the blood-guilt of the
Crucifixion. It should not be forgotten that literary interpretations may take fictive form, and that fictions, wrongly or carnally read, may prey upon life.

I have been skipping across millennia of interpretation only
to make the point that texts upon which a high value has
been placed become especially susceptible to the transformations wrought by those who seek spiritual senses behind the
carnal, senses that may in their turn be treated as if they were
carnal. All such operations require the interpreter to practice a
grandiose neglect of portions of the text. I ignored much of the
text of *Party Going*, exactly as the bulk of the Jewish scriptures
was ignored. I neglected, or treated as trivial, pretty well everything apart from the occult structure I believed myself to have
divined; which is just what the early exegetes did to the Old
Testament, preserving it only because it cast shadows important to the perceiving eye, emitted signals intelligible to the
understanding ear. Sometimes it appears that the history of
interpretation may be thought of as a history of exclusions,
which enable us to seize upon this issue rather than on some
other as central, and choose from the remaining mass only
what seems most compliant.

So I treated earlier readers of *Party Going* as having been,
like the Israelites, men in shadow, possessing a text that only
seemed to be intelligible, for the means of interpretation had
not yet become available. Such a text is an oracle that comes
true only in circumstances quite unforeseeable, to be heard
by later ears and divined by a later magic. And every text may
be treated thus. It may have some sense that can be sought

only at some long temporal remove. This was well known to those who opened the Bible or Virgil at random to discover their destinies in the first line to meet their eye. And, as I say, it is assumed by all who suppose that they, from where they stand, can best see and perceive, hear and understand, a text that has occupied interpreters for hundreds, perhaps thousands of years. They all work under the protection of some god who has a special tenderness for latent, or spiritual, senses. Let us now look at some of them interpreting parables, and ask what it means to be an insider, and what it is that keeps the carnal outsiders outside.

II

Hoti's Business:
Why Are
Narratives Obscure?

He did not speak to them without a parable.
Mark 4:34

He settled Hoti's business.
Browning, "A Grammarian's Funeral"

IF WE WANT to think about narratives that mean more and other than they seem to say, and mean different things to different people, with a particularly sharp distinction drawn between those who are outside and those who are inside, we can hardly do better than consider the parables.

A parable is, first, a similitude. "With what can we compare the kingdom of God, or what parable shall we use for it?" (Mark 4:30): here the word for parable — *parabolē* — could as well be translated "comparison," and sometimes is. It means a placing of one thing beside another; in classical Greek it means "comparison" or "illustration" or "analogy." But in the Greek Bible it is equivalent to Hebrew *mashal*, which means "riddle" or "dark saying," but I gather it can extend its range to include "exemplary tale." Sometimes the Greek word is also used to translate *hidah*, meaning "riddle."

Riddle and parable may be much the same: "Put forth a riddle and speak a parable to the house of Israel," says Ezekiel, proposing the enigma or allegory of the eagle of divers colors and the spreading vine (17:2f). The saying of Jesus that nothing that enters a man from outside can defile him is called by Mark a parable; it is not especially dark, but dark enough to call for an explanation.

What is interesting about parables from the present point of view is first this range of senses, which seems to reflect pretty well all the possibilities of narrative at large. At one end of the scale there is a zero point, a strong saying, perhaps, with no narrative content to speak of; and at the other is the well-formed story which, as structuralist exegetes like to demonstrate, exhibits all the marks of narrativity. But there is another scale to consider. Parables are stories, insofar as they *are* stories, which are not to be taken at face value, and bear various indications to make this condition plain to the interpreter; so the other scale is a measure of their darkness. Some are apparently almost entirely transparent; some are obscure.

All require some interpretative action from the auditor; they call for completion; the parable-event isn't over until a satisfactory answer or explanation is given; the interpretation completes it. In this respect it is like a riddle, sometimes a very easy riddle, sometimes one of the comic kind that contain interpretative traps: for example, the riddle that asks how you fit five elephants into a Volkswagen, which can only be answered if you ignore the hint that it has to do with size; it has to do only with number.[1] But it is more usually a tragic riddle, like that proposed by the Sphinx to Oedipus — if you can't answer it, you die, for that is the fate of the outsider who sees without perceiving and hears without understanding. Or we might try another comparison, and say that the interpretation of parable is like the interpretation of dreams, for the dream-text, when understood, disappears, is consumed by its interpretation, and ceases to have affective force (or would do so, if one were able to conceive of a completed dream-analysis).

But this notion, that interpretation completes parable, and there's an end, is much too crude. The parable of the Good Samaritan, to which I'll return, ends with a question: "Which of these three, do you think, proved neighbor to the man who fell among thieves?" There is only one possible answer: "The Samaritan." Or so it would appear to common sense; though common sense is not our business. The answer may leave an interpreter unsatisfied, because a narrative of some length, like the Good Samaritan, works hard to make the answer obvious and in so doing provides a lot of information which seems too important to be discarded, once the easy act of completion is performed.

When parable stretches out into short story commentators sometimes say that it has escaped from the genre altogether; so they call The Good Samaritan and The Prodigal Son "example stories." But that, in my view, is dodging. They are indeed parables, though as far from the pole of maxim or riddle as one can get; they are about to merge into long narratives, which may also retain some of the qualities of parable. Think, for instance, of *Party Going*. Of course between these extreme points — the maxim and the short story — there occur parables of varying degrees of "narrativity" and varying degrees of opacity. Moreover there is a relation between these properties: "narrativity" always entails a measure of opacity.

FOR THE LAST century or so there has been something of a consensus among experts that parables of the kind found in the New Testament were always essentially simple, and always had the same kind of point, which would have been instantly taken by all listeners, outsiders included. Appearances to the contrary are explained as consequences of a process of meddling with the originals that began at the earliest possible moment. The opinion that the parables must originally have been thus, and only thus, is maintained with an expense of learning I can't begin to emulate, against what seems obvious, that "parable" does and did mean much more than that. When God says he will speak to Moses openly and not in "dark speeches," the Greek for "dark speeches" means "parables." John uses a different word for parable, but uses it in just the same sense: "speak in parables" is the opposite of "openly proclaim." If a word can cover so many things, from proverbial wisdom to dark sayings requiring recondite rabbinical explanation, and even to secret apocalyptic signs, it seems likely that people who used the word in this way must have interpreted all narrative with a comparable variety and range.

In our own time we cannot easily use the word "parable"

in such a way as to exclude the notion of "enigma." Who would deny Kafka the right to call his anecdote of the leopards a parable (Gleichnis)?[2] "Leopards break into the temple and drink to the dregs what is in the sacrificial pitchers; this is repeated over and over again; finally it can be calculated in advance, and it becomes part of the ceremony." Webster (third edition, 1961) says that a parable is "a short fictitious story from which a moral or spiritual truth can be drawn." Do we draw any such truth from Kafka's parable? What, to mention first a rather minor difficulty, are we to make of those definite articles: *the* temple, *the* sacrificial pitchers? They imply that the cultus is one with which we ought to be familiar; we ought to know the god whom the temple serves, and what liquid is contained in the pitchers. Of course we don't. All we can suppose is that some familiar rite is being intruded upon, and that the intrusion is assimilated, the cultus altered to accommodate it, in a manner often discussed by sociologists of religion. The alternative procedure, to their way of thinking, would be to shoot ("nihilate") the leopards.

Beyond that, we are left to consider the peculiar nature of the rite. There are ceremonies which claim to enact an his-torical sequence of events that occurred at a particularly sig-nificant moment in the past, and to do so in such a way as to translate them into the dimension of liturgy. The Passover is such a ceremony, and so is the Eucharist; both include exposi-tions of the recurring symbolic senses of the original events. But here the repetitiveness belongs in the first place to the original events ("this is repeated over and over again") and only later becomes liturgical; though it might be argued that the presence of the leopards is all the more a Real Presence. At this point, it must be admitted, we are very close to what might be called "wild interpretation."

Here I will interpolate a reading of the parable by another hand, my wife's. "The letter of the parable," she writes, "mas-ters our freedom to interpret it. The words, we know, must mean more and other than they say; we would appropriate their other sense. But the parable serenely incorporates our spiritual designs upon it. The interpreter may be compared to the greedy leopards. As their carnal intrusion is made spiritual, confirming the original design of the ceremony, so is this figurative reading pre-figured; only complying with the sense, it adds nothing of its own and takes nothing away. In comparing himself to the leopards, the reader finds himself, unlike the leopards, free — but free only to stay outside. Thus dispossessed by his own metaphor, excluded by his very desire for access, he repeatedly reads and fails to read the words that continue to say exactly what they mean."

This reading, which firmly excludes speculation about liturgy or ritual, has, I think, much to be said for it. Thurber, peering into a microscope, saw his own eye, which was wrong; interpreters, often quite rightly, tend to see the Problem of Interpretation. The sense of the parable, on the view just stated, must be this: being an insider is only a more elaborate way of being kept outside. This interpretation maintains that interpretation, though a proper and interesting activity, is bound to fail; it is an intrusion always, and always unsuccessful. This is bewildering, for we fear damnation and think it unfair, considering how hard we tried. The opinion of Mark is quite similar: he says that the parables are about everybody's incapacity to penetrate their sense. Of course both the interpreters in question go some way toward exempting themselves from this general inhibition.

There is a famous parable in Kafka's *The Trial*. It is recounted to K by a priest, and is said to come from the scriptures. A man comes and begs for admittance to the Law, but is kept out by a doorkeeper, the first of a long succession of doorkeepers, of aspect ever more terrible, who will keep the man out should the first one fail to do so. The man, who had assumed that the Law was open to all, is surprised to discover the existence of this arrangement. But he waits outside the door, sitting year after year on his stool, and conversing with the doorkeeper, whom he bribes, though without success. Eventually, when he is old and near death, the man observes an immortal radiance streaming from the door. As he dies, he asks the doorkeeper how it is that he alone has come to this entrance to seek admittance to the Law. The answer is, "this door was intended only for you. Now I am going to shut it." The outsider, though someone had "intended" to let him in, or anyway provided a door for him, remained outside.

K engages the priest in a discussion concerning the interpretation of this parable. He is continually reproved for his departures from the literal sense, and is offered a number of priestly glosses, all of which seem somehow trivial or absurd, unsatisfying or unfair, as when the doorkeeper is said to be more deserving of pity than the suppliant, since the suppliant was there of his own free will, as the porter was not. Nevertheless it is claimed that the doorkeeper belongs to the Law, and the man does not. K points out that to assume the integrity of the doorkeeper, or indeed that of the Law, as the priest does, involves contradictions. No, replies the priest: "it is not necessary to accept everything as true, one must only accept it as necessary." "A melancholy conclusion," says K. "It turns lying into a universal principle." [3]

"Before the Law" is a good deal longer than any biblical parable, and reminds us that in principle parable may escape restrictions of length, and be, say, as long as *Party Going*. And like Mark's Parable of the Sower, it incorporates very dubious interpretations, which help to make the point that the would-be interpreter cannot get inside, cannot even properly dispose of authoritative interpretations that are more or less obviously wrong. The outsider has what appears to be a reasonable, normal, and just expectation of ready admittance, for the Law, like the Gospel, is meant for everybody, or everybody who wants it. But what he gets is a series of frivolous and mendacious interpretations. The outsider remains outside, dismayed and frustrated. To perceive the radiance of the shrine is not to gain access to it; the Law, or the Kingdom, may, to those within, be powerful and beautiful, but to those outside they are merely terrible; absolutely inexplicable, they torment the inquirer with legalisms. This is a mystery; Mark, and Kafka's doorkeeper, protect it without understanding it, and those outside, like K and like us, see an uninterpretable radiance and die.

Let me now return to Mark's formula of exclusion, which I quoted near the beginning of the book. Jesus is preaching to a crowd, teaching them "many things in parables." The first is the Parable of the Sower. He went out to sow; some of his seed fell by the wayside and was eaten by birds; some fell on stony ground, where it grew without rooting and was scorched by the sun; some fell among thorns, which choked it; and some fell on good ground, yielding at harvest thirty, sixty, and a hundredfold. "He that hath ears to hear, let him hear": this is the formula that tells you the enigmatic part of the text is concluded, and you need to start interpreting. Later, the Twelve, baffled, ask Jesus what the parable means. He replies that they, his elect, know the mystery of the kingdom and do not need to be addressed in parables, but those outside are addressed only thus, "so that seeing they may see and not perceive, and hearing they may hear but not understand, lest at any time they should turn, and their sins be forgiven them" (Mark 4:11–12). He adds, a little crossly, that if the Twelve can't make out this parable they will not make out any of them, but nevertheless goes on to give them an interpretation. What the Sower sows is the Word. People by the wayside hear it, but Satan (the birds) comes and takes it from their hearts. The stony ground signifies those who receive the Word with gladness, but are unable to retain it under stress and persecution; the thorns stand for those who hear it but allow it to be choked by worldly lust and ambition. The last group are those who hear and receive the Word and bear much fruit (4:14–20).

All this is very odd; the authorized allegory seems inept, a distortion après coup,[4] as bad as the priest's exegeses in Kafka. It gives rise to suggestions that Mark did not understand the parable, that its original sense was already lost, and its place taken by an inferior homiletic substitute. But let us put that question aside and look at the general theory of parable pronounced on this occasion: To you has been given the secret of the kingdom of God, but for those outside everything is in parables, so that they may indeed see but not perceive, and may hear but not understand; lest they should turn again and be forgiven. Some argue that Mark's so that or in order that, the Greek hina, is a mistranslation of a word that in the lost Aramaic original meant in that or in such a manner as, so that Mark's Greek distorts the true sense, which is something like: I have to speak to them in parables, seeing that they are the kind of people who can take stories but not straight doctrine. This is an attempt to make *hina* mean "because," a very desirable state of affairs. In this altered form the theory no longer conflicts with the prefatory remark that Jesus was *teaching* the crowd, which seems inconsistent with his telling stories in order to ensure that they would miss the point. It also fits the run of the sentence better: the Twelve don't need parables, but the crowd does. Apparently Mark misunderstood, or used *hina* carelessly or in an unusual way; and it is a fairly complex word. But the best authorities do not accept these evasive explanations, a refusal all the more impressive because they would really like to. They admit that Mark's *hina* has to mean *in order that;* and we are left with a doctrine described by one standard modern commentator as "intolerable," [5] by Albert Schweitzer as "repellent," and also, since the meaning of the parables is "as clear as day," unintelligible.[6]

Now it happens that Mark's first interpreter was Matthew (I assume throughout that Mark has priority and is Matthew's principal source, though this long-established position is now under challenge). And Matthew also seems to have found Mark's *hina* intolerable. For though he does not omit the general theory of parable from his big parable chapter (13), he substitutes for *hina* the word *hoti,* "because." This is a substantial change, involving a different grammar; Matthew replaces Mark's subjunctive with an indicative. Later he had to deal with Mark's *mēpote,* "*lest* they should turn," which obviously supports the uncompromising mood of *hina;*[7] here he went to work in a different way. The whole passage about hearing and seeing comes from Isaiah (6: 9–10), though Mark, in paraphrasing it, does not say so. What Matthew does is to quote Isaiah directly and with acknowledgment, so that the lines retain a trace of their original tone of slightly disgusted irony at the failure of the people to perceive and understand. The sense is now something like: As Isaiah remarked, their stupidity is extremely tiresome; this seems the best way to get through to them. The *mēpote* clause is thus bracketed off from the rest; instead of Mark's uncompromising exclusions — outsiders must stay outside and be damned — Matthew proposes something much milder: "I speak to them in parables *because* they see without perceiving..." He was, it appears, unhappy with the gloomy ferocity of Mark's Jesus, who is also, in this place, very hard on the Twelve: "if you don't understand this you won't understand anything." Matthew leaves this out, and substitutes a benediction: "Blessed are your eyes, for they see..."

It has been argued that Matthew's *hoti* has a causal force, that he is saying something like: It is only because the people lack understanding that the parables will have the effect of keeping them from the secrets of the kingdom.[8] The implication is that the exclusion arises not from the speaker's intention, but from the stupidity of his hearers, so that the blame is theirs. This gives the parables the same effect as they have in Mark's theory, while avoiding his candid avowal that the telling of them was designed to have that effect. I must leave *hoti's* business to the grammarians, but it seems safe to say that Matthew's principle of secret and inaccessible senses, if he had one, is a good deal softer than Mark's. When he came to edit Mark's concluding note ("he said nothing to them without a parable," 4:34) Matthew adds that Jesus in so doing was fulfilling the Psalmist's prophecy: "I will open my mouth in parables, I will utter what has been hidden since the foundation of the world" (Matt. 13:34–35; Ps. 78:2). And in support of this preference for overt proclamation, Matthew omits the remainder of Mark's sentence quoted above: "but privately to his own disciples he explained everything." *Ereugomai*, the verb translated as "utter" in Matthew's quotation, means "disgorge, vomit forth, spew out" and can only suggest total disclosure. On the other hand, it is Matthew who remarks, at the moment when he is explaining the difference between insiders and outsiders (13:12) that "to him who has will more be given ... but from him who has not, even what he has will be taken away," a saying used by Mark later on in the parallel chapter, and in a different context. So Matthew's position is hard to define, though we can say it was less intransigent than Mark's. It is sometimes suggested that from this moment of the ministry Jesus has given up trying to get himself understood by the Jews,[9] whom he therefore does not mind baffling. Whether this is true or not, we can say we have two kindred but different secrecy theories. Each of them makes the parable a bit like a riddle in a folktale, where to get the answer wrong means perdition; but *hina* and *hoti* distinguish them. One says the stories are obscure on purpose to damn the outsiders; the other, even if we state it in the toughest form the language will support, says that they are not necessarily impenetrable, but that the outsiders, being what they are, will misunderstand them anyway.

Now if you think that Jesus could not possibly have thought of his parables as riddles designed to exclude the masses from the kingdom; and if you have also the prior knowledge that the original parables cannot have been allegorical — so that, quite apart from this particular allegory being so feeble, you know it should not be there at all — then you are virtually obliged to claim that the whole Marcan passage is inauthentic or corrupt. Since A. Jülicher set the tone of modern parable criticism at the end of the nineteenth century, this has been the general view. According to Jülicher, Mark simply misunderstood the parable as he had it from the tradition. There are many explanations of how he might have come to do so; but behind them all is a conviction that the parables must originally have been simple illustrations of the teacher's point, made in order to help those who had difficulty with abstractions. The purpose of the Sower parable, as many think, was, like that of most of the parables, eschatological: it had to do with the end-time that had now come upon the world, with the breaking-in of the kingdom of God, here represented by the harvest, a traditional figure for it. Between sowing and harvest many frustrations occur; but when the harvest comes, and the angel puts in his sickle, all will be fruition and triumph. For this original, Jewish, eschatological sense, Mark substitutes his feeble, Hellenistic, homiletic allegory. His theory of impenetrable narrative darkness is likewise an error. Jesus occasionally made despairing observations, and Mark, somehow misled, took this one from its proper place and attached it to a group of parables with which it has nothing whatever to do.[10]

One can't help thinking of Kafka's parables as recalling these clerical contentions. Kafka, like Mark, or the text of Mark as we have it, supports what might be called the *hina* doctrine of narrative. The desire to change *hina* to *hoti* is a measure of the dismay we feel at our arbitrary and total exclusion from the kingdom, or from the secret sense of the story, of which we learn — by its radiance — only that it is overwhelmingly important. Both Mark and Kafka go on to offer unacceptable priestly glosses on their parables. Each seems to arrive at a melancholy conclusion. Matthew took the first step toward reducing the bleak mystery of Mark's proposals; and later a rational, scientific scholarship spirited away the enigma by detecting behind the text of Mark a version more to its liking.

Of course what the scholars say is plausible. They speak of a redactor living after the time when the Kingdom was imminently expected, so that he had lost the original eschatological sense of the story. He remodeled it in such a way that its original meaning was muddled by an incongruous interpretation. The attempts of the learned to explain away Mark's *hina* are worthy of Kafka's priest. But there it stands, and has stood for nineteen hundred years, a silent proclamation that stories can always be enigmatic, and can sometimes be terrible. And Mark's gospel as a whole — to put the matter too simply — is either enigmatic and terrible, or as muddled as the commentators say this passage is. Why, to ask a famous question, does Mark so stress the keeping of the secret of the messiahship of Jesus? One answer is that since this was an idea that developed only after the death of Jesus, Mark was forced to include it in his narrative *only* as a secret deliberately kept, concealed from all save the Twelve, and not understood by them until the end of the story. This leaves a good deal unexplained; nor is the theme of secrecy the only mystery in Mark. My present point is simple enough: Mark is a strong witness to the enigmatic and exclusive character of narrative, to its property of banishing interpreters from its secret places. He could say *hina*, even though his ostensible purpose, as declared in the opening words of his book, was the proclamation of good news to all.

THE SOWER PARABLE is the great crux. But it is not a parable that has any of the expansiveness or expressiveness of a short story; and it first occurs in the most difficult of the gospel texts. The Good Samaritan is an example of parable as extended narrative; and it occurs only in Luke (10:25–37), who is generally thought of as the most literary as well as the most genial and bourgeois of the evangelists. I will use it to comment on varieties of interpretation, and on the division between those who suppose that all stories have obscure senses and those who think this need not be so.

All the synoptics have the episode in which a lawyer or scribe asks Jesus which is the greatest commandment, though Luke changes the question to "What shall I do to inherit eternal life?" In Mark (12:28–34) and Matthew (22:34–40) the answer is an unadorned declaration of the requirement to love God and one's neighbor; Mark adds that Jesus commended the lawyer for knowing that obedience to these commandments was more important than burnt offerings and sacrifices. Luke again varies the procedure; instead of answering the lawyer's question, Jesus puts one of his own: "What is written in the law? How do you read?" Luke accepts the hint that the lawyer is testing Jesus; Mark does not say so, and indeed his report is inconsistent with the notion of a contest. Such contests often breed parables; so Luke includes one. When the lawyer gets the answer right, Jesus tells him so. But the lawyer, desiring to justify himself, said to Jesus, "And who is my neighbor?"

The answer to this question is the parable. According to Luke, it is meant to explain the sense of the word "neighbor" (*plēsion*). Naturally, being a coherent narrative, it says more than is strictly necessary to make this point. (The obligation upon narratives to do this is, by the way, a great generator of narrative senses.) A traveler is robbed and left wounded in a ditch. A priest and a Levite pass by without offering assistance, but a third passer-by goes to much trouble and expense to help the victim. He is a Samaritan — a member, that is, of a nation hated and despised by the Jews. The nature of his help is specified: he binds up the wounds, treats them with oil and wine, carries the half-dead patient on his own beast to an inn, and, having left with the innkeeper a supply of money for further care, departs with a promise to return. Which of the three travelers proved neighbor to the wounded man?

Here is a narrative that seems to be a simple exemplary tale. The detail that could be called redundant to its merely exemplary purpose may be explained away as a gesture toward realism, a way of adding the interest of verisimilitude, or even of topicality, to the folktalish triple design of the story. The Jericho road is chosen because it was a road on which such assaults were frequent. The Samaritan does all that can be done to help the man, expending his supplies, forfeiting the use of his animal, giving the innkeeper a precisely specified sum of money (enough to cater for the man's needs over many days) and, so far from thinking that he had now discharged his neighborly duty, promising to come back and finish the good work. This is how one ought to behave *now*, not in some storybook situation that vaguely impends. Perhaps the point is being made with such determined clarity because *we* need help, and ought not to be left in a ditch of incomprehension.

Yet this simple view of the story is very far from having gained universal acceptance. And in understanding why this is so we happen upon an important, if obvious, reason for the interminability of interpretation. My way of reading the detail of the parable of the Good Samaritan seems to me natural; but that is only my way of authenticating, or claiming as universal, a habit of thought that is cultural and arbitrary. My reading would certainly not have seemed "natural" to the church Fathers, for instance. The Holy Ghost does not give details merely to please or reassure; in all his works every word and every figure is charged with sense. The fate of the traveler represents the fall of the human race into the hands of demons;

he is Adam, who has left Jerusalem, the heavenly city, for Jericho, the world. The Samaritan is Christ, the inn is the Church, the promise to return the Second Coming.

To such interpreters the story is loaded with hidden meanings and although there will be a consensus as to certain of these, there is no suggestion that the process of interpretation need ever cease. The reading I've just alluded to is that of Irenaeus.[11] A gnostic allegorist proposed that the wine and oil embody an esoteric conception of *chrisma*.[12] Augustine interpreted the parable on several occasions, with some variation. The main purpose of the parable is to show the continuing care of the Samaritan (which means "Keeper"); for although all sins are remitted by baptism (the wine and oil) man is still weak, must be lifted up, tended and strengthened at the inn, which is the Church. Or, more elaborately, the wounded man is Adam, who has left heaven for the world (Jericho means the moon, the sphere of mutability) and fallen into the hands of demons, who strip him of immortality, leaving him half-dead. The priest and Levite represent the inefficacious old dispensation, the oil is hope and the wine good works; the beast is representative of the Incarnation, the inn of the Church, and the innkeeper of the apostle Paul. This interpretation, as Dodd remarks,[13] had great authority and longevity; but it was always subject to variation, the inexhaustibility of the text being greater than the authority even of Augustine. No doubt the parable has a carnal sense which does not vary materially; its spiritual sense is not so constant.

And we should reflect that interpretations of the kind I have touched upon were applied to narratives other than parables. All narrative is susceptible. For example, Augustine, interpreting the five loaves and two fishes of the first Feeding, says that the loaves are the books of Moses — they are of barley, rough outside and hard to open, but containing much nourishment; while the fish represent Christ in his characters as Priest and King. The multiplication of the loaves is the exposition of the Law in many volumes. The number of thousands of people is five because the people were under Mosaic Law. They sat on the grass because, being carnally minded, they rested on sensual things. The fragments they left were truths of hidden import, such as they were unable to receive (they took the carnal, left the spiritual). And so on.[14]

The persistence of this kind of explanation is well known; the following interpretation of the same passage was written more than a thousand years later: "By the five loaves, doctors understand the five Books of Moses which are aptly compared to a barley loaf; for a barley loaf on its outside is rough, in part, and harsh . . . yet within it is full of the purest flour . . . By the two fishes are signified the Prophets and Psalms, and the book of the Apocalypse in the New Testament, which, taken in their literal sense, are more difficult and obscure than the aforesaid books, but none the less in their mystical senses are far more fruitful. So it is with the Gospels and the Canonical Epistles of Paul; for as fishes lie hid in the waters, so the moral senses lurk hidden in these books." [15] Or the five loaves are the five wounds of Christ; the two fishes are the Virgin Mary and the penitent thief; the twelve baskets are the twelve articles of the Creed or the Twelve Apostles — "whichever you like," adds the preacher, certain that liberty of interpreting exists, though doubtless not without constraint.[16] I mention these medieval variations to illustrate a point made in my first chapter: an institutional tradition — such as that which transmitted Augustine's interpretation to medieval preachers — does not inhibit the indefinite multiplication of spiritual readings. One divination spawns another. If I say the fishes are one thing, that does not prevent your saying they are another, just as plausibly; and you may tell me, with notable liberality, that I may make them stand for anything I choose, though there will be a family or institutional resemblance between our interpretations.

Later the admissibility of such readings became an important issue in hermeneutics. There had long been a literalist opposition to free allegory, but Luther's rejection of it was decisive, and in the era of "scientific" interpretation it was rejected absolutely. Yet science also makes its assumptions. For example, it was assumed that the Parable of the Good Samaritan existed before Luke wrote it down (an assumption now

challenged, and for which there is no evidence). And of course
Luke was accused of getting it wrong.

It is true that good sense may be made of Luke's version if
we supply some historical context. For instance, the question,
"Who is my friend?" was less vague than it now sounds; certain rules of caste and race were involved. Also, by the folktale rule of three, you expect a third passer-by. Since the first
two were an Israelite priest and a Levite, you might also expect
that the third will be an Israelite layman — that the story,
written at a time when the clergy were greatly disliked, will
turn out to be anticlerical. However, by a rather shocking peripeteia, the third man turns out to be an enemy and unclean.
So the story, instead of saying that lay folk can be more charitable than parsons, a commonplace truth, extends the sense of
plēsion quite violently to include the least likely person imag-
inable, and so, by implication, everybody.[17]

This seems reasonable, but narrative is not a very reasonable
subject, and the view that this tale, however transparent it
may seem, however self-sufficient, *must* have senses less obvious than that is certainly not extinct. One modern interpreter
argues that the surface, with its blend of reassuring local detail
and folktale, conceals a sense that depends on secret allusion
to a repertory of Old Testament texts. That such repertories
existed is not in doubt, and I shall refer to them later. The
argument in this case is that so far from merely illustrating
the second commandment, the story of the Samaritan is about
the Second Coming. "Samaritan" (as Augustine seems to have
known) comes from the same root as "shepherd"; the Samaritan is the Good Shepherd. Moreover, *plēsion,* neighbor, is related to another Hebrew word meaning "shepherd"; and the
original parable, now concealed by Luke's, asked "Who is the
true shepherd?" So the lawyer asked a new question and got
the answer to an old one: the Good Shepherd, who comforts
our distress and will return hereafter. This "futuristic" escha-
tology is wholly lost in Luke's hortatory conclusion, "go and
do likewise." But science enables us to recover the true sense,
already imperceptible to Luke.[18] It happens to be quite close
to the sense proposed by the Fathers I've referred to, but the

method is of course quite different, theirs being allegorical and this being scientific. Other scientific readings bear no resemblance to patristic allegory: for example, the argument that the parable was written to justify sending a mission to Samaria.[19]

I suppose we could say that none of these interpretations leaves the parable untouched, unintruded upon, though it is easy to see that some regard it as deeply enigmatic and some do not. Those who think it enigmatic also think they can explain the enigma rather fully, as Augustine did long ago, and as Gerhardsson did only a few years back when he identified the Samaritan with the Good Shepherd. Gerhardsson says, in effect, that what he has unearthed *is* the interpretation. However, there is a fashion still more recent, which revives, in its own way, the notion that the sense of the text is inexhaustibly occult, and accessible in a different form to each and every interpreter. The object of this kind of interpretation is no longer "scientific"; one does not try, like Jeremias, to state what the narrative meant in its original, or in any later setting; one does not try to "re-cognize" it, as the more conservative hermeneutical theorists say one should. Rather one assumes, to quote an opponent of this school, that "the meaning of a text goes beyond its author not sometimes but always" and that "one understands differently when one understands at all."[20] The object of interpretation is now sometimes said to be to retrieve, if necessary by benign violence, what is called the original event of disclosure. This is the language of Heidegger; he takes the Greek word for "truth," *alētheia*, in its etymological sense, "that which is revealed or disclosed, does not remain concealed." Every hermeneutic encounter with a text is an encounter with Being as disclosed in it. For Heidegger indeed, it is the very fact that one is *outside* that makes possible the revelation of truth or meaning; being *inside* is like being in Plato's cave.[21]

Every such hermeneutic encounter is still, in a measure, historically conditioned, though now that limitation is no longer thought of just as a limitation — it is the prerequisite of interpretation, each act of which is unique, one man on one stool, so to speak, seeing what no power can withhold from him, his glimpse of the radiance, his share of what is sometimes called the "hermeneutic potential" of a text. Interpreters in this tradition sometimes think of earlier interpretations, transmitted by institutions, as having attached themselves to the original, and as having tended to close it off, lowering its potential rather as mineral deposits clog a pipe and reduce its flow. Since by their own interpretative act they discover what the parable *originally means*, they are not constricted by the conventional demand that interpretation should say what the parable *originally meant*, to its author and its first audience. What it meant and what it means are both actualizations of its hermeneutic potential, which, though never fully available, is inexhaustible.

Now that which requires to be disclosed must first have been covered, and this view of interpretation certainly implies that the sense of the parable is an occult sense. Its defenders like to say not that the interpreter illumines the text, but that the text illumines the interpreter, like a radiance. For this, as I said, is an outsider's theory. It stems ultimately from a Protestant tradition, that of the devout dissenter animated only by the action of the spirit, abhorring the claim of the institution to an historically validated traditional interpretation. It may be the end of that tradition; for I do not see how, finally, it can distinguish between sacred and secular texts, those works of the worldly canon that also appear to possess inexhaustible hermeneutic potential. (Heidegger's own exegeses of Hölderlin treat the text exactly as if it were sacred.) The tradition is that of a productive encounter between the text and the reader, illuminated by a peculiar grace or, in more secular terms, a divinatory genius, as far as possible independent of institutional or historical control. That encounter is the main concern not only of modern German hermeneutics but also, though their ways are different, of its French rivals. The method has, of course, been applied to the parables.

An interpreter working in this tradition cannot altogether free himself from historical and institutional constraints. He will try to avoid them, insofar as they are avoidable; but he cannot escape his own historicality, and he was trained in an institution. Nor can he acquire divinatory genius for the asking. The book that first made American readers familiar with the idea of hermeneutic potential was Robert Funk's *Language, Hermeneutic, and the Word of God*.[22] It is an admirable piece of exposition. Yet Funk agrees with Jeremias that the effect of the Good Samaritan story depends on the narrative shock of the discovery that the merciful traveler is a stranger, an enemy. He departs from known paths only when he conjectures that the wounded man might have preferred not to have the assistance of this unclean outcast; but this is a conjecture that owes nothing to the new hermeneutics. Although he denies the Good Shepherd interpretation, he agrees that Jesus is the Samaritan, and we the wounded man; so the Good Shepherd is there somewhere, in a sort of penumbra. There seems to be a traditional quality about this reading that is rather remote from the libertarian possibilities suggested by the speculative parts of Funk's book, and very remote from the unique and somber meditations of Heidegger on Hölderlin.

This is perhaps to say no more than that the interpreter is likely to have a touch of the dyer's hand. Thus structuralist exegesis of this parable will pass from a demonstration of its narrativity to a demonstration that Luke, as many have said before, mistook a parable of the Kingdom for a homiletic example story. And Paul Ricoeur is surely right to assume that interpretation begins where structuralist analysis ends,[23] that such analysis should be thought of as a way of facilitating divination.

I take it that The Good Samaritan sufficiently illustrates the point that a story need not be manifestly obscure to be thought by interpreters to possess that which only interpretation may disclose. I will end with a word on another parable, partly to accustom us to the existence of variants in gospel narrative, partly to make a point about allegorical interpretation that I have not had time to develop.

The Parable of the Wicked Husbandmen occurs in all three synoptic gospels, and in all three it follows a contest between Jesus and the chief priests or scribes and elders on the topic of his authority, for which he refuses explanations. The connection between the parable and this dispute is not obvious; there may not be one. Moreover the three versions differ significantly. Mark's is quite circumstantial: a man plants a vineyard, surrounded by a hedge and containing a tower and a winepress. Then he lets it to tenants and leaves the country. On his return he sends a servant to demand some of the fruit, presumably in accordance with the original contract. The tenants beat the servant and send him away. So he sends another, who is even worse treated, and then a third, whom the tenants kill, and then more, all of whom are either beaten or killed. Finally the landlord sends his only son (or his beloved son — the same word serves for both), supposing that the tenants will at least respect him. But they kill him too, hoping thereby to inherit the estate. What, in such circumstances, will the landlord do? He will come and destroy the tenants and give the vineyard to others (Mark 12:1–9).

This is a somewhat implausible narrative, but Matthew's variations (21:33–44) are not designed to help it in this respect. He develops the ending, saying that the new tenants will be of the kind who will ungrudgingly give up a proper share of the fruit; and he makes an explicit application: "the kingdom of God will be taken away from you and given to a nation producing the fruits of it" (21:43). He makes another change which I will mention later. Luke cuts out the tower, the winepress, and the hedge, and sends only three servants in advance of the son; they are maltreated but not killed, which improves the progression of the tale (20:9–18). The simplest and most elegant version is in the apocryphal Gospel of Thomas, a volume in the Gnostic library discovered at Nag Hamadi in Upper Egypt some thirty years ago (Logion 65). Thomas sends only two servants, who are beaten; then the son, who is killed. Thomas, who never appends interpretations, says nothing about the reaction of the father. In the present instance the synoptics also withhold direct interpretation, though all add, more or less clumsily, the saying about the stone that the builders rejected, which yet became the cornerstone.

The Parable of the Wicked Husbandmen looks very like an allegory, which is why the first reaction of scientific criticism was to regard it as inauthentic, as something made up in the church and read back into the gospel account. Let us suppose that there lies behind it a simple tale, very like Thomas' version. There were three emissaries, the first two beaten and the third killed. Having lost his property and his son, the landlord is now obliged to do something decisive; the synoptics give their versions of what this was. Mark has muddled this simple scenario. He sends not three but an indefinite number of messengers, and fails to make the treatment they receive more and more severe. And he puts in a good deal of unmistakably allegorical detail. The winepress, the tower, and the hedge come from Isaiah (5:1–2) where they are already allegorical; the vineyard is Israel. And when Mark describes the last messenger as the *huios agapētos* (beloved or only son) of the lord, he cannot be forgetting that he makes God use exactly these words of Jesus at the opening of his book (*Su ei ho huios mou ho agapētos*, 1:11). The allegory is now plain: God sent his prophets to Israel (not only two of them, hence the greater number of messengers); they were abused by the Israelites or their rulers; then he sent his son and they killed him, too. (This presupposes, on the part of Jesus, a foreknowledge of his own death, which is one reason why the scientific critics regard the parable as inauthentic.)

Matthew of course saw the point, and developed it. Where Mark says the son was killed, then cast out of the vineyard, Matthew says he was cast out and then killed; the Crucifixion took place outside the city wall. Luke cares less for allegory, dropping the Isaian tower; but he uses Matthew's order, first casting out, then slaying. Thomas alone shuns all allegory, contenting himself with the formulaic "Whoever has ears let him hear." But this is perhaps no more than an invitation to do the allegory yourself, if you can.

So it seems that the parable is an allegory, and has no point except as an allegory. It is more like Spenser's House of Holiness than Kafka's Leopards in the Temple. The reason why Mark put in a lot of messengers was simply that there had been a lot of prophets; to have only *three* would have obscured this point. Spenser represents the Seven Corporal Works of Mercy by seven beadsmen, not three. But if it *is* an allegory, where should licit allegorization stop? The common patristic answer is, of course, nowhere. Allegory is the patristic way of dealing with inexhaustible hermeneutic potential. And the Fathers had many successors; the notion that ancient myth as well as scripture concealed occult wisdom was as common during the European Renaissance as it was in the Hellenistic world. By contrast later scholars ask only what kind of allegory one may expect the evangelists to have inserted into a story that was not in itself allegorical at all. Then they ask what the story meant in its original form, before the salvation allegory got attached to it. Jülicher simply rejects the whole thing as inauthentic. Jeremias and Dodd say it reflects the resentment felt by Galilean tenant farmers toward their absentee foreign landlords; such landlords might, when all else failed, send their sons to collect, and the tenants might kill them in the hope of benefiting from a law that assigned ownerless property to the first claimant. They were wrong to do so, of course, and God would give the vineyard not to them but to the poor.[24] But this is only a more rationalistic allegory; it denies that the parable was originally what it certainly later became, a prophecy of the Crucifixion, and turns it into a somewhat ridiculous fable about current affairs.

In fact it seems impossible to think of the tale appearing in the gospel context simply as a tale. So the difficulty (unless we take the dissentient view that the parable as we have it is much as it always was) is merely that different interpretations have got attached in the course of time to the same parable. Paul Ricoeur thinks of interpretation as the linking of a new discourse to the discourse of the text; in a sense he treats the formal description of a narrative (as by the structuralists) as carnal, the long historical succession of interpretations as spiritual: the "form" of a parable (that which can be analyzed in terms of internal synchronic relations) is what ensures the survival of meaning after the disappearance of the original historical setting; and that meaning arises from a kind of conversation between the interpreter and the text. A parable, he says, is a fiction capable of redescribing life; its sense can never be fully closed, or this process of redescription would not be possible.[25] It is, one might add, a paradox applying to all narrative that although its function is mnemonic it always recalls different things. The mode of recall will depend in some measure on the fashion of a period — what it seems natural or reasonable to expect a text to say. This is another way of affirming that all narratives possess "hermeneutic potential," which is another way of saying that they must be obscure. The apparently perspicuous narrative yields up latent senses to interpretation; we are never inside it, and from the outside may never experience anything more than some radiant intimation of the source of all these senses.

So inveterate, so unalterable is this exclusion that it is easy to pass from saying that the outsiders are told stories because they are dull and imperceptive to saying that stories are told in order to keep the dull and imperceptive outside. And suppose that we somehow discovered that all stories were, after all, *hoti* stories. The interpreters *de métier* would, to protect their profession, to continue their privileged conversations with texts, at once strive to discredit the discovery; finally all stories are *hina* stories, even the story that they are all *hoti*.

That all narratives are essentially dark, despite the momentary radiance that attends divination, is a doctrine that would not have surprised pre-scientific interpreters. They might have offered various reasons for holding it, though usually they would have attributed the darkness of the tale to the intention of a divine author. Calvin and Pascal, close as they were to the epoch in which a presumptuous human reason would attempt to explain the mystery away, nevertheless agreed with Mark that the divine author made his stories obscure in order to prevent the reprobate from understanding them; on a kinder Catholic view, he did so in order to minimize the guilt of the Jews in refusing the gospel.[26] Even now, when so many theories of interpretation dispense in one way or another with the author, or allow him only a part analogous to that of the dummy hand at bridge, the position is not much altered; the narrative inhabits its proper dark, in which the interpreter traces its lineaments as best he can. Kafka, whose interpreter dies outside, is a doorkeeper only; so was Mark.

Mark distresses the commentators by using the word "mystery" as a synonym for "parable," and assuming that stories put questions which even the most privileged interpreters cannot answer. For example, he tells two stories about miraculous feedings. Any creative writing instructor would have cut one of them; but Mark's awkwardness can hardly be dismissed as accidental. Later the disciples are on board a boat and discover that they have forgotten to bring bread — there is only one loaf. At this point Jesus gives them an obscure warning: "beware of the leaven of the Pharisees and the leaven of Herod." Puzzled, they say among themselves, "it is because we have no bread," or "this is why we have no bread," or, maybe, "is this why we have no bread?" — the sense of the Greek is uncertain. Whatever they intend, Jesus gets angry. "Do you not yet perceive or understand? Are your hearts hardened? Having eyes do you not see, and having ears do you not hear?" They are behaving exactly like the outsiders in the theory of parable. The sign given them by the Feedings is lost on them, and unless something is done about it they will find themselves in the same position as the Pharisees, to whom Jesus has just refused any sign at all. So he takes them once more, slowly, through the story of the Feedings. Five thousand were fed with five loaves: how many baskets of fragments were left over? Twelve, they correctly reply. Four thousand, at the second Feeding, were served with seven loaves: how many baskets of fragments were left over? Seven. Well then, don't you see the point? Silence. Perhaps the disciples mistook the riddle as we do the one about the elephants: there is a strong suggestion that the answer has to do with number, but it probably doesn't.[27] Anyway, they do not find the answer. Here again Matthew does not want to leave the matter so obscure; his Jesus is much less reproachful, and also explains: "How did you fail to see that I was not talking about bread? Beware of the leaven of the Pharisees and Sadducees." ("Leaven," used figuratively, ordinarily meant something infectiously evil.) "Then they understood that he was not telling them to beware of the leaven of bread, but of the teaching of the Pharisees and Sadducees" (16:11–12). This is not perhaps very satisfactory; but the point is that Mark, with his usual severity, makes Jesus angry and disappointed, and also turns the insiders into outsiders. They cannot answer this riddle, any more than they could read the Parable of the Sower. And although this passage has been subjected to the intense scrutiny of the commentators, no one, so far as I know, has improved on the disciples' performance. The riddle remains dark; so does the gospel.

Parable, it seems, may proclaim a truth as a herald does, and at the same time conceal truth like an oracle. This double function, this simultaneous proclamation and concealment, will be a principal theme of what follows, for I shall concern myself with the radiant obscurity of narratives somewhat longer than parables, though still subject to these Hermetic ambivalences.

III

The Man
in the Macintosh,
the Boy
in the Shirt

Where the deuce did he pop out of?
Ulysses

So FAR I have been unable to represent the lot of the interpreter
as an altogether happy one. Yet the world is full of interpreters;
it is impossible to live in it without repeated, if minimal, acts
of interpretation; and a great many people obviously do much
more than the minimum. Interpretation is the principal concern of their waking lives. So the question arises, why would
we rather interpret than not? Or, why do we prefer enigmas
to muddles?

We may begin to consider the problem by thinking about
James Joyce's *Ulysses.* The institution controlling literary interpretation thinks well of the book; and I, as a reasonably
docile member of it, endorse its valuation. I have taken no part
in the exegetical labors that are the inescapable consequence;
but one doesn't need to have done that to be aware that the
work offers certain opportunities to interpreters — opportunities which, fortunately for one's younger colleagues, have every
appearance of being inexhaustible. One such is the riddle of
the Man in the Macintosh. It is, if you like, an aporia of the
kind that declares itself when a text is scrutinized with an
intensity normally thought appropriate only after institutional
endorsement. Such scrutiny may originate in an enthusiastic
cult, as it did in the present instance; and in the early stages
the establishment may be hostile to the cult. But if it decides
to take over the enterprise — as it took over Joyce studies —
it absorbs and routinizes that primitive enthusiasm. There oc-

MAN IN THE MACINTOSH, BOY IN THE SHIRT

curs a familiar transition from the charismatic to the institutional.

Let me remind you about the Man in the Macintosh. He first turns up at Paddy Dignam's funeral, in the Hades chapter. Bloom wonders who he is. "Now who is that lanky looking galoot over there in the macintosh? Now who is he I'd like to know?" And Bloom reflects that the presence of this stranger increases the number of mourners to thirteen, "Death's number." "Where the deuce did he pop out of? He wasn't in the chapel, that I'll swear." The newspaper reporter Hynes doesn't know the man either, and following a conversational mix-up records his name as M'Intosh. The stranger is thus given a spurious identity, a factitious proper name, by the same hand that distorts Bloom's by calling him Mr. Boom — a diminution of identity.

Later, in "The Wandering Rocks," a number of people are recorded as having taken note of or ignored the procession of the Lord Lieutenant. For example, Mr. Simon Dedalus removed his hat; Blazes Boylan offered no salute, but eyed the ladies in the coach; and "a pedestrian in a brown macintosh, eating dry bread, passed swiftly and unscathed across the viceroy's path." Why "unscathed"? Did he pass very close to the wheels? Is the Lord Lieutenant peculiarly dangerous to such persons? In "Nausicaa" Bloom, wondering who the "nobleman" may be who passes him on an evening stroll, again remembers the man, and now seems to know more about him, for he obscurely reminds himself that the man has "corns on his kismet," which may mean "is famous for being unlucky." Appearing yet again at the end of "The Oxen of the Sun," Mackintosh is described — though once more the sense is dubious — as poor and hungry. He is drinking Bovril, a viscous meat extract from which one makes a hot bouillon that is held to be fortifying, though preferred, in the ordinary way, by people of low income, and perhaps a plausible supplement to dry bread. Perhaps the stranger's eating habits are telling us something about him; perhaps we are to read them as indices of social standing and character. Yet it appears that Mackintosh has a grander cause for sorrow than simple poverty and habitual bad luck; for we are told that he "loves a lady who is dead." This might explain his presence at the funeral as well as his dietary carelessness and his reckless transit across the path of the viceroy.

He next turns up in a more positive, though phantasmagoric role; at the foundation of Bloomusalem in "Circe" he springs up through a trapdoor and accuses Bloom of being in truth Leopold M'Intosh, or Higgins, a notorious fire-raiser. Bloom counters this further threat to his already shrunken and distorted identity by shooting M'Intosh; but later the man is observed going downstairs and taking his macintosh and hat from the rack, which understandably makes Bloom nervous. And sure enough he returns; but only at the end of the novel, in the "Ithaca" section, when Bloom, meditating the pattern of the day's events, or their lack of it, hears the timber of the table emit a loud, lone crack, and returns in his musings to the enigma of M'Intosh. Not for long, however; as he puts out his candle he is reminded of another and far more ancient enigma: "Where was Moses when the candle went out?"

It can be argued [1] that MacIntosh is susceptible of explanation in terms of the known relations between Joyce's book and the *Odyssey* of Homer. He represents Homer's Theoclymenos, a character who turns up in the fifteenth book as an outlaw getting free passage with Telemachus, and then again, rather mysteriously, in the twentieth book, when the suitors, having mocked Telemachus for saying he won't coerce his mother into marrying one of them, suddenly grow sad. At this point "the godlike Theoclymenos" offers a comment on their behavior, and a dire prophecy. He tells the suitors that their faces and knees are veiled in night, that there is a sound of mourning in the air, that the walls are splashed with blood and the porch filled with ghosts on their way to Hades. The effect of these observations is to restore the good humor of the suitors, and no more is heard of the godlike outlaw.

One possible, though severe, opinion of the Homeric Theoclymenos is that his prophecy is banal and his presence in the story quite without point — in fact, that he is simply an intrusion, and does not belong to the poem at all. Can this be said to justify the presence of MacIntosh in *Ulysses*? One would then have to explain how the relevance of MacIntosh is established by the irrelevance of Theoclymenos. Certainly, however, they have something in common. MacIntosh's making the extra man and bringing the total of mourners to thirteen, and the occurrence of the funeral in the Hades chapter, chime with the funereal tone of the prophecy in Homer.

But there is still a lot left to explain. Perhaps Joyce, now imitating another famous precursor, was at his exercise of putting particular persons into his book, as Dante put certain people, in his case people of importance, into hell. So it has been proposed that MacIntosh is really a man called Wetherup, who is actually mentioned twice in *Ulysses* (with his name misspelled) and represented as given to the utterance of platitudes, though not as wearing a macintosh. Note also that MacIntosh is identified, by some scholars, with Mr. James Duffy, a character in Joyce's story "A Painful Case," which is to be found in *Dubliners*. Mr. Duffy is a shadowy wanderer and the lover of a dead woman. He illustrates what Joyce called "the hated brown Irish paralysis"; if he really is the man in the macintosh it is appropriate that Bloom should forget all about him as soon as he climbs into Molly's bed. What is more, Duffy is partly based on Joyce's brother Stanislaus, who was puritanical about sex, and argued that its absence made friendship between man and man, and its presence friendship between man and woman, equally impossible. Stanislaus was aware that James had him in mind when he invented Mr. Duffy, for he declared that Duffy was "a portrait of what my brother imagined I should become in middle age." [2]

Joyce vouched for none of this, but we know he liked jokes and riddles, and that he sometimes teased his admirers by asking them "Who was the man in the macintosh?" Another view of the whole matter is that MacIntosh is absolutely gratuitous and fortuitous, a mere disturbance of the surface of the narrative. So Robert M. Adams, who says that Joyce is just playing with our "unfulfilled curiosity," and that if the identification of MacIntosh with Wetherup, or presumably one of the other tedious possibilities I have outlined and some that I have not (for instance, that MacIntosh is Joyce himself), is correct, then "we may be excused for feeling that the fewer answers we have for the novel's riddles, the better off we are." Adams is persuaded that in the texture of this novel "the meaningless is deeply interwoven with the meaningful" so that "the book loses as much as it gains by being read closely." [3]

I daresay there is a larger literature on this drab enigma than I have suggested — certainly there could be: why, for instance, the epidemic of misspelled names? [4] — but this is enough to be going on with. The real question is, why do we want to solve it anyway? Why does the view of Adams commend itself to us not at once, not as intuitively right, but as somehow more surprising and recondite than the attempts to make sense of MacIntosh? Why, in fact, does it require a more strenuous effort to believe that a narrative lacks coherence than to believe that somehow, if we could only find out, it doesn't?

Here is a cryptic and far from wholly satisfactory answer: within a text no part is less privileged than the other parts. All may receive the same quality and manner of attention; to prevent this one would need to use metatextual indicators (typographical variation, for instance) and there are no such indicators in the present instance. Why is this so? There must be supra-literary forces, cultural pressures, which tend to make us seek narrative coherence, just as we expect a conundrum to have an answer, and a joke a point. Our whole practice of reading is founded on such expectations, and of course the existence of genres such as the pointless joke and the deviant conundrum depends upon the prior existence of the normal sort. Just so do detective stories depend upon the coherence of elements in an occult plot that declares itself only as the book ends. There are detective novels, of which Robbe-Grillet's *Les Gommes* is the supreme example, which disobey this convention; but far from disregarding it, they depend upon it for their effect. In short: just as language games are determined by historical community use, so are plot games; and the subversion of the values of either depends on the prior existence of rules.

It is a prior expectation of consonance, the assumption that as readers we have to complete something capable of comple-

tion, that causes us to deal as we do with the man in the macintosh. We look for an occult relation (since there is no manifest relation) between all the references to him. It may be hidden in Homer, or in the larger body of Joyce's writing, or in
his life, or in some myth; for we may well decide that Mac-
Intosh is Death, or even that he is Hermes. Only when we are
exhausted by our unprofitable struggle with the dry bread, the
Bovril, the corns, the charge that Bloom himself is M'Intosh,
do we relapse into a skepticism which is willing to entertain the
notion of Robert Adams' nude emperor. We come to rest somewhere in the end, for the incoherence of the evidence can induce real anxiety. Perhaps, then, the appearances of MacIntosh
lack coherence because they mime the fortuities of real life;
that relates to another of our conventional expectations of narrative. Perhaps its satisfaction may sometimes entail the use
of incoherences, devices by means of which, as Adams expresses it, the work of art may "fracture its own surface." [5]

There are current at present much bolder opinions than this
one, which presupposes, rather conventionally, that some or
much of a text can and should be processed into coherence,
though some, if after careful interpretative effort it resists this
treatment, may be left alone, or dealt with in a different way.
One bolder view would be that an ideal text would be perfectly
fortuitous, that only the fractures are of interest; that in establishing coherence we reduce the text to codes implanted in our
minds by the arbitrary fiat of a culture or an institution, and
are therefore the unconscious victims of ideological oppression.
Freedom, the freedom to produce meaning, rests in fortuity, in
the removal of constraints on sense. Insofar as *Ulysses* is not
a congeries of MacIntoshes it falls short of the ideal, though a
determined reader may do much to correct it by resisting the
codes. Newly liberated from conventional expectations first
formulated by Plato, solidified by Aristotle, and powerfully re-
inforced over the past two centuries, we are no longer to seek
unity or coherence, but, by using the text wantonly, by inatten-
tion, by skipping even (every time you read *A la Recherche du
temps perdu* it can be a new novel, says Roland Barthes, because you skip different parts each time[6]), by encouraging in

ourselves perversities of every sort, we produce our own senses. The reason why Adams could give the establishment a bit of a shock without going anywhere near these Utopian extremes is simply that Joyce studies, and kindred literary researches, were already institutionalized — a paradigm was established, "normal" research was in progress, to adapt Thomas Kuhn's terms[7] — so that even to propose that normal exegesis should be withheld from certain passages in *Ulysses* was unorthodox enough, close enough to the revolutionary, to cause a stir.

LET US NOW turn to the Boy in the Shirt (*sindōn*, a garment made of fine linen; not precisely a shirt, rather something you might put on for a summer evening, or wrap a dead body in, if you were rich enough). The Boy (actually a young man, *neaniskos*) is found only in Mark (14:51–52). At the moment of Jesus' arrest, says Mark — and Matthew agrees — all the disciples forsook him and fled. And both agree further that his captors then led him to the high priest. But between these two events Mark alone inserts another: "And a young man followed him, with nothing but a linen cloth about his body; and they seized him, but he left the linen cloth and ran away naked." And that is all Mark has to say about this young man.

The difficulty is to explain where the deuce he popped up from. One way of solving it is to eliminate him, to argue that he has no business in the text at all. Perhaps Mark was blindly following some source that gave an inconsistent account of these events, simply copying it without thought. Perhaps somebody, for reasons irrecoverably lost, and quite extraneous to the original account, inserted the young man later. Perhaps Matthew and Luke omitted him (if they had him in their copies of Mark) because the incident followed so awkwardly upon the statement that *all* had fled. (It is also conjectured that the Greek verb translated as "followed," *sunēkolouthei*, might have the force of "continued to follow," though all the rest had fled.[8]) Anyway, why is the youth naked? Some ancient texts omit the phrase *epi gumnou*, which is not the usual way of saying "about his body" and is sometimes called a scribal corruption; but that he ran away naked (*gumnos*) when his cloak was removed is not in doubt. So we have to deal with a young man who was out on a chilly spring night (fires were lit in the high priest's courtyard) wearing nothing but an expensive, though not a warm, shirt. "Why," asks one commentator, "should Mark insert such a trivial detail in so solemn a narrative?"[9] And, if the episode of the youth had some significance, why did Matthew and Luke omit it? We can without difficulty find meanings for other episodes in the tale (for instance, the kiss of Judas, or the forbidding of violent resistance, which makes the point that Jesus was not a militant revolutionist) but there is nothing clearly indicated by this one.

If the episode is not rejected altogether, it is usually explained in one of three ways. First, it refers to Mark's own presence at the arrest he is describing. Thus it is a sort of reticent signature, like Alfred Hitchcock's appearances in his own films, or Joyce's as MacIntosh. This is not widely believed, nor is it really credible. Secondly, it is meant to lend the whole story verisimilitude, an odd incident that looks as if it belongs to history-like fortuity rather than to a story coherently invented — the sort of confirmatory detail that only an eyewitness could have provided — a contribution to what is now sometimes called l'effet du réel. We may note in passing that such registrations of reality are a commonplace of fiction; in their most highly developed forms we call them realism. Thirdly, it is a piece of narrative developed (in a manner not unusual, of which I shall have something to say later) from Old Testament texts, notably Genesis 39:12 and Amos 2:16. Taylor, with Cranfield concurring, calls this proposition "desperate in the extreme."[10] I suppose one should add a fourth option, which is, as with MacIntosh, to give up the whole thing as a pseudo-problem, or anyway insoluble; but although commentators sometimes mention this as a way out they are usually prevented by self-respect and professional commitment from taking it.

Now we have already noticed that Mark, for all the boldness of its opening proclamation ("The beginning of the good news of Jesus Christ") is, to say the least, a reticent text, whether its reserve is genuinely enigmatic or merely the consequence of muddle. Moreover, as I have suggested, where enigmas are credibly thought to exist in a text, it is virtually impossible to maintain that some parts of it are certainly not enigmatic. This is a principle important to the history of interpretation, and it was by carefully violating it with his fractured-surface theory that Robert Adams upset people. Let us then look at two attempts that have been made to treat the boy in the shirt as enigmatic and functional.

The first of these very well illustrates one alarming aspect of the business of interpretation, which is that by introducing new senses into a part of the text you affect the interpretation of the whole. And this "whole" may be not simply Mark, but the history of early Christianity. It has lately been shown that there was more than one version of Mark. Morton Smith found, in a Judean monastery, an eighteenth-century Greek manuscript in which was copied a letter written by Clement of Alexandria at the end of the second century. After demonstrating that this letter was indeed written by Clement, Smith studies a passage in it that purports to be a quotation from Mark, though it is nowhere to be found in the gospel as we have it. The context is as follows: Clement is commending his correspondent Theodore for taking a firm line with the Carpocratian Gnostics, a contemporary libertine sect which believed it right to sin that grace might abound; indeed they were "unafraid to stray into ... actions whose very names are unmentionable," as Irenaeus, speaking of Carpocatians and Cainites alike, reports.[11] Now Clement wishes to distinguish his authentic secret Mark from the inauthentic and conceivably licentious secret Mark of the Carpocratians. He explains that Mark first wrote his gospel in Rome, drawing on the reminiscences of Peter (we know from other evidence that Clement, like most other people, accepted this account of the origin of the gospel). But on that occasion Mark left out certain secrets. After Peter's martyrdom, says Clement, Mark went to Alexandria, where he "composed a more spiritual gospel" for the exclusive use of those who were "being initiated into the great mysteries." Carpocrates had presumably taken over this secret gospel and adulterated it with his own interpretations. In the circumstances, says Clement, it will be best for the faithful to deny the very existence of a secret version.

He then quotes a passage from the authentic Alexandrian version. It must have come somewhere in the present tenth chapter of the gospel, and it tells of a visit to Bethany. In response to the plea of a woman, Jesus rolled back the door of a tomb and raised a rich young man from the dead. The young man, looking upon him, loved him, and begged to be with him. After six days he was commanded to go to Jesus at night. This he did, wearing a linen garment (sindōn) over his naked body (epi gumnou). During the night Jesus instructed the young man in "the mystery of the kingdom of God." Then the text continues at 10:35 as we now have it.

Clement goes out of his way to deny that the true, as distinct from the spurious, secret text contains the words gumnos gumnou, which might suggest that the master as well as the catechumen was naked. Whether this suggestion bore on baptismal practice, or had other magical and sexual import, is a matter for conjecture in the light of what is known of Carpocratian habits; for of course if Clement is telling the truth the words have no place in his genuine text, only in the spurious version of Carpocrates.

In Morton Smith's opinion the initiation in question was baptism. The story of the young man raised from the dead is obviously related to that of Lazarus, which occurs only in John, and Smith believes they have a common original older than the Mark we now have. He also thinks that our young man in the linen shirt is this same young man in Clement's gospel who had looked and loved and worn a sindōn over his naked body. In the extant gospels Jesus never baptizes, but in Clement's version of Mark baptism must have been a central rite; and Clement would want to preserve this initiation ceremony from contamination by the libertine Gnostics. Anyway, the young man in Mark's account of the arrest is on his way to be baptized; that is why he is naked under his sindōn, a garment appropriate to symbolic as well as to real burial, and appropriate also to symbolic resurrection, both to be enacted in the ceremony. His baptism would take place in a lonely garden, under cover of night. We know that Jesus set guards (on this theory, to prevent interruption) and we know that the guards fell asleep. He was then surprised with the naked youth.

Thus the entire narrative is altered to make sense of a part of it. But the account I have so far given is a very inadequate account of Smith's hypothesis. He also proposes the view that the secretiveness of Mark's Jesus almost throughout the gospel is related to this use of baptism as initiation into the mysteries of the kingdom. Jesus is here regarded as a magician or shaman, the Transfiguration is explained as a shamanistic ascent. Now the Gnostic libertine interpretation of the secret gospel can be seen as an attempt to preserve or recover an original mystery concealed by the expurgated "Roman" version of Mark in general circulation. Like Clement, only more so, the Gnostics could think of the popular text as corrupt and imperfect in consequence of its attempt to keep the secrets. And whatever may be said about the provenance of these Alexandrian secret texts, they do provide a reason why the text as we have it appears both to reveal and proclaim, and at the same time to obscure and conceal.[12]

We see, then, that an interpretation of our two Marcan verses along the lines proposed by Morton Smith entails a drastic revision of the received idea of a much larger text. We might want to ask some low-level questions about plausibility: for example, why did the hand that so expertly curtailed the tenth chapter fail to deal with the anomalous verses about the young man in the shirt? And perhaps there could be other explanations for the repetition of *epi gumnou*. This, as I said, has been thought unacceptable; it is absent from some good manuscripts at 14:51, and Taylor drops it from his text; but its recurrence in Clement's letter must mean either that it was right, and that Mark used it twice, or that whoever wrote the secret version of Chapter 10 did so with the story of the young man in mind. At any rate it seems not unlikely that in the two verses we have been considering the secret gospel is showing through, a radiance of some kind, merely glimpsed by the outsider. And we should not be unduly surprised that the gospel, like its own parables, both reveals and conceals.

It is obvious by now that the story of the young man in the shirt cannot be *simply* interpreted; and complex interpretations, whether or not they have the seismic historical effects of Morton Smith's, will always have consequences that go far beyond the local problem. The most elegant interpretation known to me is that of Austin Farrer.[13] It uses as evidence Mark's linguistic habits, but it also finds in the gospel an occult plot, this time typological in style. Farrer was writing before the discovery of Clement's letter. It would probably have changed his argument in some ways, though he would doubtless have found useful to his purposes the occurrence, in the secret Mark, of the words *neaniskos* (not the most usual word for a young man) and *sindōn*. Mark uses *neaniskos*, in the public gospel, only for the young man who fled, and for the one who, at the end of the gospel, greets the women at Jesus' empty tomb.

Behind Farrer's interpretation is the knowledge that many of the crucial events in the gospel, especially in the Passion narrative, are closely related to Old Testament texts. They fulfill these texts, and the narrative as we have it records, and is in a considerable measure founded upon, such fulfillments. More of this later; for the moment it is sufficient that an event in the gospel stories may originate, and derive some of its value from, a relationship with an event in an earlier narrative. The force of the connection may be evident only if we are aware of the conditions governing such relationships, for example that the relation of Jesus to the Law, and of Christian to Jewish history, is always controlled by the myth of fulfillment in the time of the end, which is the time of the gospel narratives. If this is granted, there is always a possibility that the sort of relationship Taylor called "desperate in the extreme" — between the story of the young man and the texts in Genesis and Amos — exists. Moreover, if the gospel contains allusions so delicate and recondite to earlier and uncited texts, why should there not be internal allusions and dependencies of equal subtlety? By seeking out such occult structural organizations one might confer upon Mark, after centuries of complaint at his disorderly construction, the kind of depth and closure one would hope to find in what has come to be accepted as the earliest and, in many ways, the most authoritative of the gospels.

Farrer's theories about Mark — numerological, typological, theological — are far too complicated to describe here, though to a secular critic they are exceptionally interesting. He himself altered them and then more or less gave them up, partly persuaded, no doubt, by criticisms of them as farfetched, partly disturbed by the imputation that a narrative of the kind he professed to be discussing would be more a work of fiction than an account of a crucial historical event. Neither of these judgments seems to me well founded. But let me say briefly what he made of the young man in the cloak. He sets him in a literary pattern of events preceding and following the Passion: for example, the unknown woman anoints Jesus at Bethany, and he says this anointing is an early anointing for burial; afterwards the women make a futile attempt to anoint his corpse. The youth who flees in his *sindōn* forms a parallel with the youth (also *neaniskos*) the women find in the tomb. The first youth deserted Jesus; the second has evidently been with him since he rose. Furthermore, the linen in which Joseph of Arimathea wraps the body is called a *sindōn*, so there seems to be an intricate relationship between the *neaniskos* in his *sindōn* and the body in the tomb, now risen. As I say, the relation might have been made still more elaborate had Farrer known of the passage in Clement, which also involves a *neaniskos* in a tomb. He tells us that the punishment of a temple watcher who fell asleep on duty was to be beaten and stripped of his linen garment; which may have a bearing on the boy's losing his. He also accepts the affiliation which Taylor rejected, believing that the young man is related to (he does not say "invented to accord with") two Old Testament types, one in Amos (2:16) — "on that day the bravest of warriors shall be stripped of his arms and run away" — and the other in Genesis (39:12), where Joseph escapes from the seduction attempt of Potiphar's wife by running away and leaving his cloak in her hands.

In such patterns as these, Farrer detected delicate senses, many of them ironical. And since he was not an adherent of the latest school of hermeneutics, he believed that Mark must have intended these senses, and that he must have had an audience capable of perceiving them. So far from being a bungler, awkwardly cobbling together the material of the tradition, Mark developed these occult schemes "to supplement logical connection," by which I take it Farrer meant something like "narrative coherence." He let his imagination play over the apparently flawed surface of Mark's narrative until what Adams calls fractures of the surface became parts of an elaborate design.

I do not doubt that Farrer's juggling with numbers gets out of hand. But even that has a basis in fact. He was confronting a problem that earlier exegetes had experienced. Since there is certainly a measure of arithmological and typological writing in the New Testament (twelve apostles and twelve tribes, Old Testament types sometimes openly cited, sometimes not) is there not reason to think that intensive application may disclose more of it than immediately meets the eye? Yet the more complex the purely literary structure is shown to be, the harder it is for most people to accept the narratives as naively transparent upon historical reality.

At one point Farrer even suggests that the young man deserting is a figure representing the falling off of all the others. This seems to me a fine interpretation. We have, at this moment in the narrative, three principal themes: Betrayal, Flight, and Denial. Judas is the agent of the first and Peter of the third. I shall have more to say of Judas as Betrayal in Chapter Four. Peter, halfway through the gospel, was the first to acknowledge the Messiah, though the acknowledgment was at once followed by a gesture of dismissal by Jesus: "Get behind me, Satan — you care not for the things of God but the things of man." Now he apostasizes and perhaps even curses Jesus,[14] exactly at the moment when his master is for the first time asserting his true identity and purpose before the Sanhedrin. The implication, first made at the moment of recognition, and followed by the first prophecy of the Passion, is that the chief apostle will, when the Passion begins, deny the master. On both occasions he stands for the wholesale denial of Jesus, almost for Denial in the abstract. So too this young man, who is Desertion. The secret passage enhances this reading; the typical deserter is one who by baptism or some other rite of initiation has been reborn and received into the Kingdom. Nevertheless he flees. Thus we may find in this sequence of betrayal, desertion, and denial, a literary construction of considerable sophistication, one that has benefited from the grace that often attends the work of narration — a grace not always taken into account by scholars who seek to dissolve the text into its elements rather than to observe the fertility of their interrelations. It must, however, be said again that these narrative graces entail some disadvantages if one is looking more for an historical record than for a narrative of such elaborateness that it is hard not to think of it as fiction.

How do the interpretations of Smith and Farrer differ? The first assumes that Mark built up an esoteric plot, using material that was somehow also available to John, who developed it differently in the story of Lazarus and his sisters. The second argues that Mark worked an existing Passion narrative, presumably quite simple, into a complex narrative structure so recherché that between the first privileged audience and the modern interpreter himself no one ever understood it in its fullness. The frame of reference of the first is provided by the techniques of historiography, that of the second by literary criticism. Each is in its own way imaginative, though the quality of imagination differs greatly from one to the other. A Schweitzer might place Smith's work in the tradition of lives of Jesus, beginning two centuries ago with Bahrdt and Venturini,[15] which assumed that what made sense of the gospel narratives was something none of them ever mentioned: for example, that Jesus was the instrument of some secret society. As to Farrer, his work was rejected by the establishment, and eventually by himself, largely because it was so literary. The institution knew intuitively that such literary elaboration, such emphasis on elements that must be called fictive, was unacceptable because damaging to what remained of the idea that the gospel narratives were still, in some measure, transparent upon history.[16]

The constructions of Smith are historical; those of Farrer are literary. But they both assume that there is an enigmatic narrative concealed in the manifest one. Each suggests that an apparent lack of connection, the existence of narrative elements that cannot readily be seen to form part of a larger organization, must be explained in terms of that hidden plot, and not regarded as evidence of a fractured surface, or mere fortuities indicating that reality may be fortuitous. Joyce once said of *Ulysses*: "I've put in so many enigmas and puzzles that it will keep the professors busy for centuries over what I meant, and that's the only way of ensuring one's immortality." [17] This is a shrewd joke, but the suggestion that enigmas and puzzles have necessarily to be "put in" is false. Joyce was only imitating the action of time. It would be more accurate to say that whatever remains within the purview of interpretation — whether by the fiat of the professors or of some other institutional force — will have its share of enigmas and puzzles. Whatever is preserved grows enigmatic; time, and the pressures of interpretation, which are the agents of preservation, will see to that. Who was the man in the macintosh? Mr. Duffy, Stanislaus Joyce, Mr. Wetherup, Bloom's doppelganger, Theoclymenos, Hermes, Death, a mere series of surface fractures? Each guess requires the construction of an enigmatic plot, or, failing that, a declaration that the text is enigmatically fortuitous. Who was the boy in the linen shirt, and where did he pop out of? The answers are very similar: a candidate for baptism, an image of desertion, a fortuity that makes the surface of narrative more like the surface of life.

So I return to the question I have already put: why do we labor to reduce fortuity first, before we decide that there is a way of looking which provides a place for it? I have still no satisfying answer; but it does appear that we are programmed to prefer fulfillment to disappointment, the closed to the open. It may be that this preference arises from our experience of language-learning; a language that lacked syntax and lacked redundancy would be practically unlearnable. We depend upon well-formedness — less so, it must be confessed, in oral than in written language: in the written story there is no visible

gesture or immediate social context to help out the unarticu-
lated sentence, the aposiopesis. There are modern critics who
think our desire for the well-formed — or our wish to induce
well-formedness where it is not apparent — is in bad faith.
They hold that it is more honest to experience deception, disappointment, in our encounters with narrative. They have not
yet prevailed; we are in love with the idea of fulfillment, and
our interpretations show it. In this we resemble the writers of
the New Testament and their immediate successors, who were,
though much more strenuously, more exaltedly, in love with
fulfillment; the verb meaning to fulfill, and the noun *pleroma*,
full measure, plenitude, fulfillment, are endlessly repeated, and
their senses extend from the fulfillment of prophecy and type
to the complete attainment of faith.

Such expectations of fullness survive, though in attenuated
form, in our habitual attitudes to endings. That we should
have certain expectations of endings, just as we have certain
expectations of the remainder of a sentence we have begun to
read, has seemed so natural, so much a part of things as they
are in language and literature, that (to the best of my knowledge) the modern study of them begins only fifty years ago,
with the Russian Formalist Viktor Shklovsky. It was he who
showed that we can derive the sense of fulfilled expectation, of
satisfactory closure, from texts that actually do not provide
what we ask, but give us instead something that, out of pure
desire for completion, we are prepared to regard as a metaphor
or a synecdoche for the ending that is not there: a description
of the weather or the scenery, he says, will do,[18] say the rain
at the end of Hemingway's *Farewell to Arms*, or the river at
the end of Matthew Arnold's *Sohrab and Rustum*. These are
matters that still require investigation; the fact that they do so
testifies to the truth of the statement that we find it hardest to
think about what we have most completely taken for granted.

Now it happens that Mark is never more enigmatic, or never
more clumsy, than at the end of his gospel; and I can best bring
together the arguments of this chapter by briefly considering
that ending. Too briefly, no doubt; for whole books have been
written about it, and it has been called "the greatest of all liter-

ary mysteries." [19] It is worth saying, to begin with, that nobody thought to call it that until after Mark had come to be accepted as the earliest gospel and Matthew's primary source; we do not recognize even the greatest literary mysteries until the text has gained full institutional approval. When Mark was thought to derive from Matthew it was easy to call his gospel a rather inept digest, as Augustine did; and then the abruptness of the ending was merely an effect of insensitive abridgment, and not a problem at all, much less a great mystery. Even now there are many who are impatient of mystery, and wish to dispose of it by asserting that the text did not originally end, or was not originally intended to end, at 16:8. But very few scholars dare to claim that the last twelve verses, 9–20, as we still have them in our Bibles, are authentic, for there is powerful and ancient testimony that they are not.

The gospel we are talking about ends at 16:8. In the previous verse the young man in the tomb gives the women a message for Peter and the disciples concerning their meeting with the risen Jesus. But they flee the tomb in terror and say nothing to anybody. This ending must soon have come to seem strange, which is why somebody added the extra twelve verses. We are not entitled to do anything of that kind; we can argue that the gospel was, for some reason, left unfinished; or we can interpret the ending as it stands.

The last words of the gospel are: "for they were afraid," *ephobounto gar*. It used to be believed that you could not end even a sentence with such a construction; and to this day, when it is accepted that you could do so in popular Greek, nobody has been able to find an instance, apart from Mark, of its occurrence at the end of a whole book. It is an abnormality more striking even than ending an English book with the word "Yes," as Joyce did. Joyce's explanations of why he did so are interestingly contradictory. *Ulysses*, he told his French translator, "must end with the most positive word in the human language." [20] Years later he told Louis Gillet something different: "In *Ulysses*," he said, "to represent the babbling of a woman as she falls asleep, I tried to end with the least forceful word I could possibly find. I found the word *yes*, which is

barely pronounced, which signifies acquiescence, self-abandon-
ment, total relaxation, the end of all resistance." [21] Here again
Joyce gives the professors a license to interpret which they
would have had to take anyway. The only positive inference
to be made from these two remarks is that Joyce knew, as
Shklovsky did, that we all want to make a large interpretative
investment in the end, and are inclined to think the last word
may have a quite disproportionate influence over the entire
text. Later he ended *Finnegans Wake* with the word *the;* in
one sense it is as weak as Mark's enclitic *gar,* though in another it is definite though barely pronounced, and deriving
strength from the great *ricorso,* which makes it the first word
in the book as well as the last. These ambiguities are not unlike
those of Mark's problematical ending.

Let us pass by the theories which say the book was never
finished, that Mark died suddenly after writing 16:8, or that
the last page of his manuscript fell off, or that there is only one
missing verse which ties everything up (such a verse in fact
survives, but it is not authentic and will probably not be in
your Bible), or that Mark had intended to write a sequel, as
Luke did, but was prevented. Let us also skirt round the more
congenial theory of Jeremias, that Mark went no further because he thought that what happened next should be kept from
pagan readers.[22] We can't deny that this fits in with a pattern
of revelation and deception observable elsewhere in Mark; nor
that there is evidence of secrets reserved to the initiate, or expressed very cryptically, as in Revelation. Still, it's hard to see
why the gospel, which is a proclamation of the good news,
should stop before it had fairly reached the part that seemed
most important to Paul; by Mark's time it had been preached
for an entire generation.

So let us assume that the text really does end, "they were
scared, you see," and with *gar* as the last word, "the least forceful word" Mark "could possibly find." The scandal is, of course,
much more than merely philological. Omitting any post-Easter
appearance of Jesus, Mark has only this empty tomb and the
terrified women. The final mention of Peter (omitted by Matthew) can only remind us that our last view of him was not as

a champion of the faith but as the image of denial. Mark's book began with a trumpet call: "This is the beginning of the gospel of Jesus Christ, the son of God." It ends with this faint whisper of timid women. There are, as I say, ways of ending narratives that are not manifest and simple devices of closure, not the distribution of rewards, punishments, hands in marriage, or whatever satisfies our simpler intuitions of completeness. But this one seems at first sight wholly counter-intuitive, as it must have done to the man who added the twelve verses we now have at the end.

A main obstacle to our accepting "for they were scared" as the true ending, and going about our business of finding internal validation for it, is simply that Mark is, or was, not supposed to be capable of the kinds of refinement we should have to postulate. The conclusion is either intolerably clumsy; or it is incredibly subtle. One distinguished scholar, dismissing this latter option, says it presupposes "a degree of originality which would invalidate the whole method of form-criticism." [23] This is an interesting objection. Form-criticism takes as little stock as possible in the notion of the evangelists as authors; they are held to be compiling, according to their lights, a compact written version of what has come to them in oral units. The idea that they shaped the material with some freedom and exercised on the tradition strong individual talents was therefore foreign to the mode of criticism which dominated the institution throughout the first half of the present century. And that alone is sufficent to dispose of the idea as false. Now all interpretation proceeds from prejudice, and without prejudice there can be no interpretation; but this is to use an institutional prejudice in order to disarm exegesis founded on more interesting personal prejudices. If it comes to a choice between saying Mark is original and upholding "the whole method of form-criticism" the judgment is unhesitating: Mark is not original. To be original at all he would have had to be original to a wholly incredible extent, doing things we know he had not the means to do, organizing, alluding, suggesting like a sort of ancient Henry James, rather than making a rather clumsy compilation in very undistinguished Greek.

Yet if we look back once more to the beginning of Mark, we might well have the impression that this brief text, so much shorter than any of the other gospels, at once gave promise of both economy and power. First, an exultant announcement of the subject, then the splendidly wrought narrative of John the Baptist, which, though heavy with typology, has memorable brevity and force. It is a world away from the overtures of the other gospels. Matthew and Luke were not content with it, perhaps it did not seem a true beginning, this irruption of a hero full grown and ready for action; so they prefixed their birth stories and genealogies. We are so used to mixing the gospels up in our memory into a smooth narrative paste that laymen rarely consider the differences between them, or reflect that if we had only Mark's account there would be no Christmas, no loving virgin mother, no preaching in the temple — nothing but a clamorous prologue, the Baptist crying in the wilderness, with his camel-skin coat and his wild honey. Matthew and Luke started earlier, with Jesus' ancestry, conception, and birth; John exceeded them both, and went back to the ultimate possible beginning, when, in the pre-existence of Jesus, only the Word was.

Mark, it appears, could not maintain this decisiveness, this directness. He grows awkward and reticent. There are some matters, it seems, that are not to be so unambiguously proclaimed. The story moves erratically, and not always forward; one thing follows another for no very evident reason. And a good deal of the story seems concerned with failure to understand the story. Then, after the relative sharpness and lucidity of the Passion narrative, the whole thing ends with what might be thought the greatest awkwardness of all, or the greatest instance of reticence: the empty tomb and the terrified women going away. The climactic miracle is greeted not with rejoicing, but with a silence unlike the silence enjoined, for the most part vainly, on the beneficiaries of earlier miracles — a stupid silence. The women have come to anoint a body already anointed and two days dead. Why are they so astonished? Jesus has three times predicted his resurrection. Perhaps they have not been told? Perhaps their being dismayed and silent is no stranger than that Peter should have been so disconcerted by the arrest and trial? He knew about *that* in advance. And we might go on in this way, without really touching the question.

Farrer, extending the argument I've already mentioned, finds the answer in the double pattern of events before and after the Crucifixion. Before it, Jesus said he would go to Galilee; spoke of the anointing; gave to the disciples at the Last Supper a sacramental body which should have made it clear to them that the walling up of a physical body was unimportant. The disciples fled before the Crucifixion, the women after it. And all in all, says Farrer, the last six verses of the gospel (3–8) form "a strong complex refrain, answering to all the ends of previous sections in the Gospel to which we might expect it to answer." [24] So for him the ending, like everything else in this strange tacit text, is part of an articulate and suggestive system of senses which lies latent under the seemingly disjointed chronicle, the brusquely described sequence of journeyings and miracles. Farrer may persuade us that even if he is wrong in detail there is an ending here at the empty tomb, and it is for us to make sense of it.

Earlier, in my first chapter, I used the term "fore-understanding." It is a translation of the German word *Vorverständnis,* and its value in hermeneutics is obvious. Even at the level of the sentence we have some ability to understand a statement before we have heard it all, or at any rate to follow it with a decent provisional sense of its outcome; and we can do this only because we bring to our interpretation of the sentence a pre-understanding of its totality. We may be wrong on detail, but not, as a rule, wholly wrong; there may be some unforeseen peripeteia or irony, but the effect even of that would depend upon our having had this prior provisional understanding. We must sense the genre of the utterance.

Fore-understanding is made possible by a measure of redundancy in the message which restricts, in whatever degree, the possible range of its sense. Some theorists, mostly French, hold that a fictive mark or reference inevitably pre-exists the determination of a structure; this idea is not so remote from *Vorverständnis* as it may sound, but it is so stated as to entitle the theorist to complain that such a center must inevitably have an ideological bearing. "Closure . . . testifies to the presence of an ideology." [25] To restrict or halt the free movement of senses within a text is therefore thought to be a kind of wickedness. It may be so; but it is our only means of reading until revolutionary new concepts of writing prevail; and meanwhile, remaining as aware as we can be of ideological and institutional constraints, we go about our business of freezing those senses into different patterns. Of course the inevitability of such constraints, which increase with every increase of ideological or institutional security, is a reason why outsiders may produce the most radiant interpretations.

The conviction that Mark *cannot* have meant this or that is a conviction of a kind likely to have been formed by an institution, and useful in normal research; the judgments of institutional competence remove the necessity of considering everything with the same degree of minute attention, though at some risk that a potential revolution may be mistaken for a mere freak of scholarly behavior. But there are occasions when rigor turns to violence. The French scholar Etienne Trocmé, steeped in Marcan scholarship and the methods of modern biblical criticism, can argue that an understanding of the structure of Mark depends upon our seeing that in its original form it ended, not at 16:20, and not at 16:8 either, but at the end of the thirteenth chapter, which forms the so-called Marcan apocalypse, and immediately precedes the Passion narrative. Given the religious and political situation at the moment of writing, this is where the gospel ought to end, with an allusion to the genre of apocalypse current at that time, and a solemn injunction to watch, which refers to a particular first-century community of Christians and not to the historical narrative as such. If one accepts this position it becomes possible to show that the preceding part of the text is consonant with this ending; and what is not consonant can be explained as the work of the editor who later revised the gospel and added the Passion narrative for a "second edition, revised and supplemented by a long appendix." [26] By such means one may, without violating the institutional consensus, prepare a text that conforms with one's own rigid fore-understanding of its sense. On the other hand, Farrer's reading is condemned as it were by institutional intuition; we may therefore call it an outsider's interpretation. I find it preferable to interpretations that arise from the borrowed authority of the institutionalized corrector, and presuppose that the prime source of our knowledge of the founder of Christianity will necessarily be compliant with whatever, for the moment, are the institution's ideas of order.

Farrer's notions of order were literary, and although his tone is always reverent, and occasionally even pious, he makes bold to write about Mark as another man might write about Spenser, except that he has some difficulty with the problem of historicity, for he could certainly not accept Kant's word for it that the historical veracity of these accounts was a matter of complete indifference. Of course his motive for desiring fulfillment was related to his faith and his vocation. But his satisfaction of that desire was to be achieved by means familiar to all interpreters, and like the rest he sensed that despite, or even because of, the puzzles, the discontinuities, the amazements of Mark (and the gospel is full of verbs meaning "astonish," "terrify," "amaze," and the like), his text can be read as somehow hanging together.

If there is one belief (however the facts resist it) that unites us all, from the evangelists to those who argue away inconvenient portions of their texts, and those who spin large plots to accommodate the discrepancies and dissonances into some larger scheme, it is this conviction that somehow, in some occult fashion, if we could only detect it, everything will be found to hang together. When Robert Adams challenged this conviction he was thought bold. The French utopians challenge it in a different way, condemning the desire for order, for closure, a relic of bourgeois bad faith. But this is an announcement of revolutionary aims: they intend to change what is the case. Perhaps the case needs changing; but it is the case. We are all fulfillment men, *pleromatists*; we all seek the center that will allow the senses to rest, at any rate for one interpreter, at any rate for one moment. If the text has a great many details that puzzle us, we ask where they popped up from. Our answers will be very diverse: Theoclymenos or Stanislaus, Mr. Duffy or Death, a hooded phallus haunting tombs, a mimesis of fortuity and therefore not in itself fortuitous. Or perhaps: a candidate for baptism; a lover; a mimesis of actuality; a signature. We halt the movement of the senses, or try to. Sometimes the effort is great. Bloom failed with the man in the macintosh; the hour was late, too late for him to sort out carnal and spiritual, manifest and latent, revealed and concealed. He had had a long hard day and went, quite carnally, to bed. Perhaps he returned to the question later, as we must.

IV

Necessities
of
Upspringing

These are the fascinations of the
fabulist's art, these lurking forces of
expansion, these necessities of
upspringing in the seed, these
beautiful determinations, on the
part of the idea entertained, to
grow as tall as possible . . .
Henry James

I HAVE BEEN talking about different ways in which narratives acquire opacity, and considering some of the ways in which interpretation encounters latent senses. It appears that our interpretative zeal is normally but not always subject to regulation, that there are insiders and outsiders; that the *spes hermeneutica* is usually and even perhaps always disappointed, wherever one stands. Now I go on to consider another and very familiar source of opacity, of complex, various, and never definitive interpretation, namely character.

The relation between what is now called character and what is now called plot has been a subject of interest since Aristotle — whom for our own reasons we habitually misread — gave it his attention in the *Poetics*. My discussion begins not with Aristotle, but with a more recent theorist and practitioner, Henry James. James, in his Preface to *The Portrait of a Lady*, reports with approval the views of Turgenev on "the usual origin of the fictive picture. It began for him almost always," says James, "with the vision of some person or persons, who hovered before him, soliciting him, as the active or passive figure, interesting him and appealing to him just as they were and by what they were. He saw them, in that fashion, as *disponibles*, saw them subject to the chances, the complications of existence, and saw them vividly, but then had to find for them the right relations, those that would most bring them out; to imagine, to invent and select and piece together the situations most useful and favourable to the sense of the creatures themselves, the complications they would be most likely to produce and feel." Turgenev added that people sometimes complained of his not having enough story; but all he needed, he said, was enough to exhibit the relations of his characters. Perhaps he did lack "architecture"; but too much architecture, he surmised, was worse than too little if it interfered with what he called "his measure of the truth."

James took comfort from these sayings, for he too knew "the intensity of suggestion that may reside in the stray figure, the unattached character, the image *en disponibilité*." In the beginning, so he tells us of *The Portrait of a Lady*, there was a "single small corner-stone, the conception of a certain young woman affronting her destiny"; and this, he says, constituted "all my outfit for the large building." Such were the origins of his novels — mere germs he calls them, not *plots*, "nefarious word." And he professes to envy "the imaginative writer so constituted as to see his fable first and make out its agents afterwards." First he thinks of a presumptuous girl affronting her destiny. Only then can he get on to the business of "organising an ado about Isabel Archer." [1]

That this is an oversimplified account of James's own practice as we may study it in the *Notebooks*, that one could quote other pronouncements of James to qualify its tendentiousness, does not diminish its present value. It belongs to its period, which has not yet quite ended; it belongs also to a late moment in the history of narrative. That character, in the modern sense of the word, takes precedence over story (or "agent" over "fable") seems natural enough after two and a half centuries of the novel, and after endless practice in reading the narrative clues on which — with the help of our memories of other books, our knowledge of character codes — we found our conventional notions of individuality. Yet there is nothing natural about it; it is a cultural myth, which was deeply established when Turgenev and James spoke as they did. For Aristotle the fable came first, and character (*ēthos*, admittedly not perfectly translated by "character") followed; though this does not mean character is without importance, only that it lacks autonomy, could never originate a narrative.[2]

It would be absurd to ask whether James or Aristotle is closer to the truth. Though the latter was precluded from admitting it, character does generate narrative, just as narrative generates character. The primitive "ado" must, insofar as it is a series of actions, have agents, and these agents, insofar as ado or fable acquires extension, must transcend their original type and function, must cease to be merely Hero, Opponent, and so on, and acquire idiosyncracies, have proper names. The more elaborate the story grows — the more remote from its schematic base — the more these agents will deviate from type and come to look like "characters." The immediate motive may be realism or something else; whatever it is, the text of the story is spangled with signs that may be read as part of the evidence from which we habitually construct character.

We have all been trained to interpret, even to overinterpret, such indications of deviance from type. Schoolchildren are expected to be able to infer something called the character of Macbeth from indices scattered about Shakespeare's text. There is room for disagreement even at this level: some arrange the clues in such a way as to make up a rather noble but sadly uxorious figure; others condemn the king less unequivocally. There is institutional agreement that there exists an abstractable entity called the character of Macbeth, with which all views must conform in some measure if the candidate is to pass the examination; yet there is always the possibility of being original about the subject, for the institution urges examiners to reward originality very highly. It is curious that so small a bundle of words should not only have a highly developed internal structure, should present sequences simulating duration and causality, should impress us as a vast design, but also, as it were incidentally, throw off these more or less intemporal indices, on the basis of which we perform our character-building exercises, supplementing them by inferring from the repertoire of indices characteristics not immediately signaled in the text, but familiar from other texts and from life.

James was writing his Prefaces and according his measure of priority to character at about the time A. C. Bradley was writing his *Shakespearean Tragedy*, a work which, with some injustice, has long been condemned as a model for vicious character-interpretation. The danger is precisely that we award priority to an aspect of narrative which must in some sense always be secondary. Turgenev and James are talking about the kind of novel — made possible by the existence of a great many other novels, novels that had lost any obvious connection with primitive fable — of which it was possible to say that the narrative was generated by character, by an image *en disponibilité*, in which there was no anterior "plot" but only a germ out of which one generated an "affair." Yet not even the later novels of James, in which the subordination of plot to character is much more profound than in *The Portrait*, can support an affair quite independently of plot. There must be comings and goings and reasons for them; conversations much change the possible outcomes; Maisie's parents, by living and misbehaving rather than dying, as they did in the earliest scenario, create narrative needs. An affair is a complex of human relations. There is an Oedipus affair, and it is worked out in a complex plot; the plot has agents, and the agents have proper names, usually, though not always, the same (Jocasta, Tiresias), so that we come to think of them as characters.

Now I shall discuss a part of the Passion narrative — roughly, the Last Supper, the Betrayal, and the Arrest — as belonging to a fable of which imaginative writers, namely the evangelists, "made out the agents," in the manner of those imaginative writers whom James professed, unconvincingly, to envy. We shall also see that the clearer apprehension of those agents, subsequent to their initial making out, generates more narrative (in the phase of the operation that most interested James) and this additional narrative makes the characters increasingly *disponibles* as they free themselves from the mere necessities of their function as agents; so they call for yet more narrative, and we end with a structure that might seem susceptible of more or less endless elaboration, were it not that extraneous forces somehow put an end to the process (publication, or the award of canonical status to a particular version).

My use of the word *fable* is not meant to imply a judgment on the historicity of the narrative; nor does it necessarily imply that there was a written narrative prior to those we possess, though many, perhaps most scholars believe that there was such a document. All, I think, accept that there was a primitive version of some kind which was later elaborated, and in practice one cannot distinguish between that version and what I call the fable. The proliferation of conjectures about lost earlier versions, ur-gospels, sayings-sources, and so forth has always been a feature of the modern tradition of biblical scholarship, and of course it is in principle quite plausible to make such conjectures. Still, it strikes me as testimony to the way our minds work when confronted by a problematical text; we find it easier to think about if we imagine something *behind* it rather different from what we have in front of us. In the same way Shakespearians may find explanations of the mysteriousness, or, as they may think, the unsatisfactoriness of *Hamlet,* by considering instead the *ur-Hamlet,* though there is no general agreement about the constitution of that work, which must, in any case, be inferred from the extant versions. So biblical critics solace themselves with an Aramaic Matthew or a proto-Luke or an ur-Mark, or a Passion narrative. It is at least convenient to think of the methodologically describable *fabula* as having historical existence.

Analysts of another stripe — synchronic or "formalist" analysts — see no need to project these earlier versions on to an historic scale in order to make heuristic use of them. They may speak of a *fabula* underlying a narrative without committing themselves to the view that this fable had independent prior existence. It is a methodological fiction merely, used to help us understand the "narrativity" of the story we are considering, and, or so one hopes, to make it more accessible to a purely literary interpretation. This is dangerous ground, for the neo-Formalists would wish to disallow the second part of that program. "Can we find ourselves," I ask with Paul Ricoeur, "a position between, on the one hand, a methodological fanaticism which would forbid us to understand anything besides the method we practice, and, on the other, a feeble eclecticism which would exhaust itself in inglorious compromise?" [3] Ricoeur wants to believe that when the structural analysts have done their work, interpretation may take over. When structural analysis becomes structural*ist*, he argues, it turns ideological and begins, quite improperly, to issue bans and censures. I think he is right in this matter, at any rate up to this point, and allow myself some use of neo-Formalist terminology to say things that its inventors and proponents would certainly disapprove of.

As every schoolboy now knows, Vladimir Propp sought to demonstrate that the characters of Russian folktale could be seen as surface manifestations, or if you like secondary elaborations, of deep-lying plot functions; there were thirty-one of these functions, which could be reduced to seven "spheres of action," labeled Villain, Donor, Helper, Sought-for-Person, Despatcher, Hero, and False Hero. At the depth Propp was working there were no "characters." There was a preliminary situation, followed by a Mischief or Lack, and then by a sequence of functions that closed what the Mischief had opened.[4] There have been various attempts to make this scheme more rigorous; for example A. J. Greimas[5] speaks of six "actantial" roles, arranged in binary opposition, thus: Lord/Sought Person; Despatcher/Addressee; Helper/Opponent. A Sender communicates an Object to a Receiver, the Object being what the Receiver lacks. The Helper, working against the Opponent, realizes the wishes of the Sender in respect of the Receiver. These actants are not, and do not necessarily become, characters; thus, according to Daniel Patte,[6] in the story of the Good Samaritan the Object is Health, the Receiver is the wounded man, the Subject is the Samaritan, and the Opponent is the robbers; but the Helper is the wine and oil. In this fashion all narratives are held to be performances of which the actantial scheme represents the underlying competence.

It would be wrong to suggest that this model, of which I have given the most superficial account, has won general acceptance[7] or that it is without rivals; but it does seem to me to represent a useful way of thinking about the relation of character to narrative structure. It is a very un-Jamesian way, certainly, for it reduces every character to an actant, and an actant has no being except in relation to a plot. It may give an impression that one prefers the reductive to the expansive, to what James celebrates as "necessities of upspringing in the seed"; but the object is to read aright these very processes of expansion, of upspringing, and to understand better what James calls "beautiful determinations."

Let us then presuppose a *fabula,* progressively interpreted: first by Mark, then by Matthew and Luke[8] using Mark, and by John, who perhaps used a not dissimilar but not identical original. Whatever version of the fable Mark had before him, it was probably the only bit of consecutive narrative available to him; the gospels, in the often quoted judgment of Martin Kahler, are "passion narratives with extended introductions." [9] Of course the nature of the intermediate version, whatever it may have been, must be inferred from the "derived" narratives we actually possess, and so must the primitive fable itself, which we need not think of as having had historical existence. All we are doing is imagining what it was that the evangelists set out to interpret. I say "interpret" because the redaction of an existing narrative was, in these circumstances, a pre-exegetical interpretative act; instead of interpreting by commentary, one does so by a process of augmenting the narrative. It is quite widely agreed that the evangelists used methods continuous with those by which, before the establishment of the canon, ancient texts were revised and adapted to eliminate or make acceptable what had come to be unintelligible or to give offense. The practice is known as midrash; among other things it entailed narrative alterations or interpolations, sometimes very free. They might be made not only in the process of updating texts, but also in translating them into another language, say Greek or Aramaic. The evangelists were perfectly familiar with this practice. An unfamiliar foreign expression, or the interpretation of a difficult part of the Law, or a story which, in the course of time, had come to seem ambiguous or even indecent, such as Sarah's sojourn in the harem of the Pharaoh, might prompt midrash. Narrative explanations were provided to justify Sarah — Pharaoh knew she was married, and anyway could not work his Egyptian will on her. Or, how did it happen that Joseph married the daughter of Potiphar, an Egyptian? An Alexandrian romance maintains that the daughter was first converted; a rabbinical explanation has it that she was really the daughter of Dinah, reared by the wife of Pharaoh, but a born Jew. Thus discrepancies, or indecencies, are eliminated by the invention of romantic narrative.[10]

An Old Testament text used to support the veracity of, and given narrative interpretation in, the New Testament is called a *testimonium* or testimony. A book of testimonies was a collection of Old Testament texts brought together in a notebook for the use of preachers. Some think such books existed, in codex form for ease of reference, before any of the books of the New Testament was written.[11] The only testimony book of the right date is a collection of proof texts about the Messiah found in a cave at Qumran;[12] but the evidence that people did "search the scriptures" for proofs of the validity of Christianity is ample enough, and the existence of comparable notebooks in Christian communities, and at an early date, is a plausible assumption. It is also reasonable to suppose that narrative interpretation of the texts so collected should have had a part in the shaping of the gospel stories, including the Passion narratives. That is to say, parts of the gospel narratives may have been composed as midrashim on testimonies.

Such midrash presupposes belief in the continuing relevance of Old Testament texts, a relevance that is brought out by remodeling it, and setting it in a new narrative context, where it will enhance the truth and power of the doctrines shared by the writer and his audience. The process may be quite violent, as at Qumran, where scripture was forced into precise conformity with the history and expectations of one particular sect. The basic assumption is that the present is the end-time, when all the figures and prophecies will be fulfilled, and the new text is shaped to conform with the old; on occasion, the old may even be altered for the sake of the new.

The degree to which midrash affected the composition of the gospels remains a matter of dispute. Some bolder spirits think it of extreme importance, arguing, for example, that we need not suppose Matthew to have had any source other than Mark, since all that he adds to Mark can be accounted for in terms of midrash.[13] Luke has also been regarded as a very free practitioner of this interpretative art.[14] Others are much more cautious, disliking the idea that the interpretation of testimonies can have affected the true record; for instance Raymond Brown in his book on the Infancy Narratives expressly condemns the identification of midrash with fiction.[15] In fact there is nothing unreasonable about this identification, and a secular critic may speculate more freely about it.

At the moment I limit myself to a consideration of the generation, by interpretative means akin to midrash, of the Passion narratives as we have them, and of the characters as they developed from its agents. It is usual to describe the narrative as having five sections: Leavetaking, Arrest, Trial, Execution, and Reunion. (These are the terms used by C. H. Dodd, who even refers to the sections as "acts.")[16] But we should think of the sequence as having been constituted of two separate elements; there is, as we shall see, evidence that the primitive accounts began with the Arrest. Also early, but independent, were reports of a Last Supper, which by the time of Paul's first letter to the Corinthians had been fixed as part of the liturgical tradition; and Mark's account of the breaking of bread and drinking of wine is strongly liturgical. So the Last Supper was a fixed point for him, and in a continuous narrative it would fall most naturally immediately before the Arrest, as it does, eucharistic words included, in all the synoptics. But only from the Arrest onwards do all the versions proceed in close agreement. Jeremias, on whom I am now drawing, distinguishes a short account, which began with the arrest, and a long account, in which the material is, as he puts it, "supplemented back" to the entry into Jerusalem, and the episode of Peter's denial inserted. This long account includes, of course, the Leavetaking. Finally the evangelists filled out the story each in his own way.[17]

In Paul's account of the Last Supper we hear that it occurred "on the same night in which he was betrayed (1 Cor. 11:23). The evidence suggests that to establish continuity and connection in the narrative, the betrayal was "supplemented back" into the Leavetaking from the Arrest; or, the move from one stage of the narrative to the other (Leavetaking to Arrest) bred the function Betrayal before the agent of betrayal was identified. For the mention of Judas at the scene of the arrest is of the kind that makes him seem like someone the reader has not heard of yet. Mark and Matthew say "Judas came, one of the twelve"; Luke speaks of "the man called Judas." John's "Judas, the one betraying him" (or, "handing him over") is less relevant, for John had done much more than his predecessors to characterize Judas in earlier sequences — his "supplementing back" is more thorough, and he sounds less as if he were working from a source that here introduced Judas for the first time (Mark 14:43, Matt. 26:47, Luke 22:47, John 18:2).

We may then suppose that at an earlier stage, in what Jeremias calls the "short account," Judas had no part in the scene of the Last Supper. He was worked into it later, when he took over the function of Betrayal, so becoming the agent by which the story is moved from its first to its second "act." This belated birth of the character Judas is not contested by his single earlier synoptic appearance, in the list of the Twelve (Mark 3:19, Matt. 10:4, Luke 6:16), for there he comes at the end of the list, already labeled Betrayer, as if by another, slightly perfunctory, "supplementing back."

The necessity, in a circumstantial and history-like story, of having a character to perform the Betrayal is obvious enough. Depending how one looks at it, he plays the role of Helper or Opponent; by opposing the Hero he serves the logic of the narrative, as Satan did in Job. Satan's name means "adversary" or "opponent"; so here, when, as Luke and John report, he

entered into Judas, we have a case of a character being possessed by his narrative role. Of course by opposing he helps;
his evil act, like Satan's, is permissive, ultimately a means to
good.[18]

So Betrayal becomes Judas. In the fully formed narrative the
scheme is more complicated, for all the Twelve, and especially
Peter, are Betrayers and Deserters (prodotēs, a traitor, one who
abandons in danger), and this fact has to be got into the narrative. Moreover it is necessary, granted his supernatural powers,
that the Hero shall know he is to be betrayed, and by whom.
These needs call for new narrative, and the relative liberty of
midrashic writing ensures that each version finds a different
way of satisfying them. But all versions include the story of
Peter's denial, and Jesus' announcement that he will be betrayed by an intimate friend.

This announcement is, quite typically, constructed on an
Old Testament text, one of many used in the Passion narrative; and like many of the others it comes from the Psalms:
"Even my bosom friend, whom I trusted, who ate of my bread,
betrays me" (41:9). This text is the "germ" of the scene; and
from it grows also the episode that precedes the narrative of
the meal: Judas' visit to the chief priests, and his offer to betray Jesus. His decision to do so raises the further question,
why should he wish it? It is the kind of question that helps
to turn a plot-agent into a character. The probable answer is,
for money; and so the character begets more narrative.

How did Mark develop the narrative of the meal itself?[19]
When Jesus announces that one of his table companions will
betray him, the Twelve are sorrowful, and each asks, "Is it I?"
Whereupon Jesus cries woe upon the traitor, though he does
not name him. There follows the liturgical narrative of the
bread and wine.[20] We note that the bread, now augmented by
wine, retains a connection with the original testimony; the
figure of betrayal becomes one with the figure of ritual sacrifice, as if to suggest that the two are inseparable.

After the meal they set out for the Mount of Olives. In
Mark the independent movement of Judas, who must have
left on his own to join the posse that will arrest Jesus, is not

chronicled; Judas is next mentioned at the moment of the arrest. The kiss betrays; it is an inversion of the holy kiss that would have followed the sacred meal; betrayal, not sacrifice, is consummated. This may be a highly developed narrative interpretation of the testimony. And for Mark, that is the end of Judas. He has done his narrative part. So in this gospel there is not a great deal to distinguish Judas from a more abstract agency — he might be called simply "the Betrayer," or "Betrayal," as in some morality play; indeed, we may be reminded of the manner in which, in some of those plays, the personae fluctuate between the condition of named persons and that of mere abstractions, between King Johan and Rex.

But there is already enough of Judas to ensure that there will be more, when the work of narrative interpretation continues, and the character takes shape. Matthew, we assume, had Mark open before him as he wrote. How did he interpret these scenes? Well, whereas Mark merely reported the visit of Judas to the chief priests, Matthew records the dialogue that took place on that occasion: "What will you give me if I deliver him to you?" The answer is, thirty pieces of silver. Matthew invented this sum of money, but for him invention almost always follows a set form. His view of what might have happened is under the control of his respect for the Old Testament repertoire of messianic prophecies and figures; so he finds his thirty pieces of silver in Zechariah (11:12): "They weighed for my price thirty pieces of silver."

There is no evident consonance between the context of this passage in Zechariah and Matthew's new use of it. And although this silver sounds a plausible price — in the ordinary way passes the test of narrative plausibility — it is important to see that it belongs, in a sense, to another plot altogether, a plot founded on occult connections between the new narrative and many old ones, a plot not at all dependent on sequentiality or plausibility. There may be a constellation of texts, of which the new one is the essential illuminant, that which confers an ultimate, unsuspected meaning. But since this is a narrative, such consonances have to be inserted into the syntagmatic flow. So Matthew finds himself embarked on a subplot. He remembers two texts in Jeremiah: in the first the prophet buys a flask at the potter's house and breaks it at the burial ground, as a sign that the kings have filled Jerusalem with innocent blood; in the second he buys a field for seventeen shekels of silver. Matthew's Judas confesses that he has betrayed the blood of the innocent, and casts his silver into the Temple (this is from Zechariah's "I cast them into the Lord's house"). Since such money could not be received in the Temple, the chief priests use it to purchase the potter's field to bury strangers in. Matthew, in 27:9–10, spells out the connection with Jeremiah with the customary fulfillment citation. But there may be others, not so indicated. Some believe that when Matthew wrote the story of Judas' treachery he remembered Achitophel, who, having betrayed David, set his house in order and hanged himself (2.Sam. 17:23),[21] as Judas sets his house in order by returning the guilty money; and others think he may have been remembering the brothers of Joseph, who sold him for twenty shekels of silver (Gen. 37:28).

From his Old Testament material Matthew makes vivid narrative (and vivid dialogue: "What is that to us? See thou to that") though it is not, on close examination, very plausible; for instance, Judas is returning the money in a place to which he can hardly have had access, and to men who, as we know, are busy elsewhere, in the praetorium. The death of Judas also creates problems. The account of it given in Acts (1:16–20) is different from Matthew's (he fell headlong, and his bowels gushed out). There is yet another account, preserved by Papias, which says that Judas swelled up to such a size that a place where a wagon could pass was too narrow for him. This makes his death resemble those traditionally reserved for tyrants and very wicked men, like Herod the Great. Elsewhere there are reports that Judas lived on to see the Resurrection, and then burst. It was long ago proposed that the three principal traditions had each a scriptural source: Matthew's we know; Acts used a passage in Wisdom (4:17ff); and the Papias tradition used 2 Maccabees (9:7–18) and perhaps other sources, all describing the deaths of wicked men.[22]

All this (and there is much more of it) suggests not only the deepening complexity of Matthew's interpretation of Mark, but the freedom with which the Betrayer was characterized by the addition of detail far in excess of the minimum required for the narrative realization of Betrayal. Are we to find this of interest only with regard to scriptural narrative? I think not. Such narrative has of course its peculiarity: the Old Testament and the Apocrypha are treated as a sort of seminary of narrative germs, which are transplanted and grow into the history-like story of the Passion. And although the actual repertoire employed may be presumed to have been somehow restricted to a central corpus of messianic texts, augmented by others at need — as Zechariah, who had already provided Matthew with the figure of the Shepherd, now contributes the thirty pieces of silver — it may be said that in principle any Old Testament text had a narrative potential that could be realized in the New Testament. One might well suppose such an arrangement to be without parallel; but it is not altogether unlike the relation obtaining between the early pages of a long novel and its later pages. The earlier ones contain virtualities or germs, not all of which grow; there is a mass of narrative detail, existing in its own right and, like the Old Testament, viable without later "fulfillment," though it may be fulfilled. A special kind of novel, the classic detective story, actually depends on our ability to distinguish, like the witches in *Macbeth*, which seeds will grow and which will not, sometimes puzzling us by making one kind look like the other.

The novel, exploiting such intermittent fulfillments, is a form of narrative inconceivable as anything but a book in the modern sense; it requires, in principle, that we be able to turn back and forth in its pages. A novel written on a roll would be something else. So it is of interest that the Christians, from a very early date, preferred the codex to the roll. The Jews, upon whom the end of time had not come, whose prophecies of a Messiah were unfulfilled, kept the roll, but the Christians, having the desire to establish consonance between the end of the book and the beginning, needed the codex, and not only used it for their own books but transferred the Old Testament to the same form.[23] Just how early they made the change is, as I have said, debated; but it is at least possible that Mark first circulated in codex. These early codices could not contain the whole Bible, but they still made for much greater ease in reference back; a new view of the history of the world entailed a new system of retrieving and ordering information about it. The transfer of the Hebrew scriptures to Greek codices enacts the appropriation of those writings for Christian purposes. It made possible the use of the Jewish account for the peculiar purpose of establishing the validity of the Christian version not by, or not only by, reference to the Law and the Prophets, but also by reference to the testimonies, scattered apparently at random in the ancient texts, and having occult senses that only now emerged. Thus the Old Testament becomes the basis for an enormous peripeteia; one finds in its *chronos* prefigurations of the *kairoi* manifested in the New.[24] So the codex, originally perhaps the memorandum-books of Hellenistic businessmen, became the vehicle for a new kind of narrative, reflecting new views on the divine and human arrangement of time. In its way the novel perpetuates that archaic confidence in the figural relation of the new event to the old, in continuities of sense ever to be renewed and re-established, and in the expectation, however qualified, that the end must cast its potent shadow over all that precedes it. The book, then, is a permanent image of occult design and coherence; consonances can be written into it, if necessary by altering what occurred in the first place (as occasionally happened in early Christian versions of the Old Testament) or more usually by shaping what occurs in the second place, as when Matthew incorporates discrete passages from the Jewish Bible into his account of Judas.

It cannot have seemed to him, as he wrote his midrash on Mark's Judas story, that he was simply inventing. There was the image of Judas, *en disponibilité;* intense suggestions as to its disposal were already present in the book to which he was adding. It was all part of the business of being a writer, and Matthew is generally thought to have been a more skillful writer than Mark, though it is proper to add that there is more to writing than so restricted a notion of skill implies. Certainly he was neater than Mark. For example, he sees no reason for referring twice, as Mark does, to the testimony about the bread; once was better, and he cut the first one out. He is quick, too, to spot gaps in Mark's narrative, spaces he also held to be *en disponibilité*. When Jesus prophesies that one of the Twelve will betray him, Mark makes them all ask, "Is it I?" In Matthew it is Judas alone who asks the question; and he gets the characteristic reply *su eipas*, "Thou hast said so," the same answer that Jesus will make to Pilate when asked if he is King of the Jews (*su legeis*), and the same that he makes to the High Priest when asked if he is the Christ. (That is the point at which Mark's hero, in general much more reticent, very surprisingly says *egō eimi*, I am. Matthew either had a variant text,[25] or wanted to eliminate what must have struck him as an inexplicable irregularity, or valued the triple repetition more highly than Mark's narrative shock.)

Su legeis can mean anything from "Yes" to "That's what *you* say" or "No comment"; but in Matthew's new Judas scene it adds to Mark a full recognition, by the hero, of the Opponent/Helper. So the fable grows at once more complex and more explicit. What is odd is that Matthew, having instituted this promising development, does nothing more with it. Nobody, it seems, overhears what is said between the two, though there is no hint that it was said in secret. The story, after this new crisis, simply goes on as before, and Judas, having presumably gone off on his own, turns up next at the arrest, freshly identified as "one of the twelve." He says "Hail, master!" and kisses Jesus. What Jesus says next is variously translated: "Friend, why are you here?" or "Friend, wherefore art thou come?" or "Friend, do what you are here to do"; or, on the assumption that the vocative *hetaire* should be translated not as "O friend" — as it normally would be — but as a prelude to a reproach, as elsewhere in Matthew, there are versions such as Moffatt's "My man, do your errand." I have not enough Greek to adjudicate between these versions of the cryptic original,[26] but there may be a tendency in these later versions to cover up an inadequacy or bald spot in Matthew's narrative.

Certainly the simpler translations make very odd reading, especially since Matthew repeats the Marcan "My betrayer is at hand." It is as if the recognition scene at supper had never been played; as if Matthew had forgotten what he had just written.

Anyway, Matthew says no more about Judas until he interpolates into the developing story of the Passion a new account of what became of the betrayer in the end. He gives back the blood money and then commits suicide. Nothing but an interest in character can account for these narrative additions. There was an original need of narrative, and it was supplied by narrative interpretation of the testimony. But narrative begot character, and character begot new narrative. In the course of these developments, new gaps may be inevitable. This is how interpretation works in fiction.

Luke mostly follows Mark, or follows what Mark follows, quite closely, making the kiss quite explicitly the moment of recognition. That the fable offered further possibilities to the narrative interpreter is made very clear by John. As I mentioned, all the evangelists associate Judas with betrayal when they first name him in the list of the Twelve; John, however, provides a more detailed prefiguration of the betrayal: "Did I not choose you twelve, and one of you is a devil? He spoke of Judas . . . for he was the one that would betray him, being one of the Twelve" (6:70–71). John picks up this demonic theme (to which Luke also alludes, 22:3) at the beginning of his leavetaking scene: "During supper, when the devil had already put it into the heart of Judas Iscariot, Simon's son, to betray him" (or, "The devil had already made up his mind that Judas . . . should betray him"). After the washing of the feet, which is in John alone, Jesus predicts his betrayal. In doing so he makes no mention of the testimony of the bread, from Psalms 41:9. The Twelve look uncertainly at one another. Peter then asks the Beloved Disciple, who is "lying close to the breast of Jesus," that is, reclining next to him, to find out who is to be the traitor. The Beloved Disciple has no proper name; obviously it was not Peter; it has even been proposed that it was Judas, an excellent midrash. He passes on the question to Jesus, who replies, "It is he to whom I shall give this morsel when I have dipped it." And he gives it to Judas.

This is a beautiful transformation, into vivid narrative — all the more so if indeed he hands the bread to the man who asked the question — of the testimony cited by Mark and Matthew, and now, as a text, evaporated altogether. As Judas eats the morsel he receives Satan into him, so that the eucharistic bread appears in a demonic inversion, and Satan, the Opponent/Helper, is incorporated into the human agent. This is the fullest recognition, and the consequences may follow at once: "What you are going to do, do quickly." And John, who has already done so much to thicken the narrative texture, now fills another gap in Matthew's account by considering the reaction of the remaining ten of the Twelve. They heard some of what was said, but did not know why it had been said. (The handing of the dipped morsel would be taken as a normal part of the ceremony of the meal.) Some conjectured that as treasurer of the party Judas was being sent out to buy more food, or to give alms to the poor (a customary activity on Passover night, though in John, the Leavetaking does not occur on that night,[27] as we shall see). John has prepared the reader for this earlier, by designating Judas as the treasurer — as it happens, dishonest — of the group. Only in John is Judas specified as the one who complains about the extravagance of the expenditure on ointment at Bethany; in the other versions of that scene (which are interestingly different in other respects also) there is only a general grumble.

By this time the scene of leavetaking and recognition is dense with narrative suggestion, and John cannot simply move on from it, as the synoptics did; he cannot leave Judas with the rest of them, he must send him out. "So, after receiving the morsel, he immediately went out. And it was night." The Greek is terser: *exēlthen euthus; ēn de nux.* This "immediately," *euthus,* happens to be a favorite word of Mark's — he uses it forty times in his short gospel, and it imparts to his narrative a sort of restlessness, of nervous random movement. Here, in John, it sounds quite different; it has an abrupt finality. That the last words should be "it was night" may remind us of what Shklovsky said about the use of such expressions to procure narrative closure.[28] At any rate, what we have here is a remarkably refined bit of narrative, in its fullness a world away from Matthew and two worlds away from Mark, where all remained *disponible*. We feel close to the novel. Not that the process is all filling and expansion; there is also an economy of means. The words "what you are going to do, do quickly," and the abrupt departure of Judas, do the work of Matthew's thirty pieces of silver, and make redundant any account of his future remorse and death.

So if we compare these transformations of the fable, we are bound to think of Matthew's as more highly developed than Mark's, and John's than Matthew's. Mark is characteristically spare, a grid rather than a plenum; it is his strength, though it is easier to admire John's literary skill. In much the same way Mark, having decided that the supper took place on Passover night, seems reluctant to develop the theme; whereas John, perhaps the bolder and more resourceful writer, decides against Passover night and gets everything he can out of the changes consequent on this decision. What he wanted was to make the Crucifixion coincide with the slaughter of the paschal lambs. The idea was not his, for it is expressed by Paul (I Cor. 5:7). As one scholar puts it, "the typology" came to be "understood as chronology";[29] since Christ was the Passover sacrifice he should, in narrative, be killed at the same time as the lambs, and this involved having the supper before Passover. The object of this may have been theological, but it is a decidedly literary effect, for it achieves a relation between two disparate sequences of event (the killing of the lambs and the execution of Jesus) which is, so to speak, contrapuntal. A writer who can manipulate narrative with that measure of assurance is likely to be able to give ample force and coherence to a simpler single episode, as we saw John could. Here the contrapuntal-typological effect requires John to make adjustments elsewhere in the narrative. He insists obliquely that the Passover came on the day after the Crucifixion, by saying "it was the day of Preparation for the Passover"; by pointing out that the bodies of the

crucified would have to be taken down before 6 P.M., when
Passover sabbath began; and by saying that the Jewish leaders
avoided entering the praetorium, "so that they might not be
defiled, but might eat of the Passover."

We are familiar enough with such chronological rearrange-
ments in historical novels, and indeed in Shakespeare. The
critics tell us, or used to, that in the fable that underlies *Henry
IV* there is a dim abstraction they call Riot, a Helper/Oppo-
nent who became Falstaff. The same pair of plays contains a
good deal of chronological juggling. The process by which Riot
became Falstaff is the same that turned Betrayal into Judas;
and the changes of timing are similar, too.

We may suppose that in "the primitive account" these matters were more simply presented. It is not unreasonable to conjecture that there was originally no Judas at all; that he entered
the story for the first time at the moment of the Arrest, and was
expanded backwards. Paul Winter, in his book on the trial of
Jesus, ponders the name "Iscariot." No one has ever been sure
what it meant; some say it simply refers to the place Judas
came from, others that it derives from *sicarius,* a word for
assassin (this commends itself to those who believe Jesus and
the Twelve to have been a more or less militant revolutionary
group), and some say that Mark would have explained it if he
could, but that the origin of the name had already been forgotten. Winter thinks it derives from an Aramaic word meaning Betrayal;[30] I have no competence to judge this derivation,
but you can see why I find it attractive. A function develops
into a proper name; so it becomes a character, whose life and
death have a narrative; and then the function is lost in the
character. In the first extant account it has already been forgotten that Judas Iscariot was Judas the Betrayer, and, before
that, simply Betrayal.

And once Betrayal becomes a character there is no limit to
the narrative possibilities. To some who thought that the gospel narratives distorted the true story, Judas even became a
hero, as he did in the thinking of the Gnostic sect called Cainites. Much later he continued his life in medieval tradition.

In the *Golden Legend* he is an Oedipal figure, married to his mother. There is some pity for him; it was conjectured that God called out to him, saying that he was willing to save him, but that Judas hanged himself nevertheless. The idea that Judas was acting under duress is quite common. He had a scold for a wife, and she made him steal out of the purse he kept as treasurer, and eventually she forced him to sell his master for more money. Perhaps the most interesting example of this continuing narrative embellishment is the "Ballad of Judas," a thirteenth-century work, and the oldest ballad in English. In this poem Jesus gives Judas thirty pieces of silver to buy food, warning him that he may meet kinsmen on his way. He meets his sister, who loudly condemns him for associating with Jesus; he tells her to be quiet, lest Jesus take revenge on her. But she persuades him to withdraw to a rock, and lie with his head in her lap. He falls asleep, and when he wakes the money is gone. Judas tears his hair in anguish. Then a rich Jew, named Pilate, arrives, and asks Judas if he will sell his Lord. Only for the thirty pieces of silver that are Jesus' own, Judas replies. Then the scene shifts abruptly to the Last Supper. Jesus tells the Twelve that he is bought and sold for food. Judas asks, "Is it I?"; and Peter affirms that not Pilate nor ten hundred knights would prevent his fighting in defense of his lord. With the prophecy of Peter's denial the ballad suddenly ends.

John is behind, but a long way behind, this version. The idea that Judas is acting under constraint, and perhaps involved in an incestuous relation with his sister, represents an active form of treachery, while Peter, without the same duress, represents a passive one, is presumably a free development. So is the subplot in which the money obtained by selling Christ is provided by himself, so that the bread which represents his body, or is transformed into it at the Eucharist, is actually obtained by the sale of that body. Thus the crime of Judas makes possible the Mass. This, and other medieval stories which tell us that Judas lost the money gambling, are very far from Matthew, who invented his pieces of silver for quite other purposes. The new narrative generated by the character is governed by a different set of interests. The ballad is a fair example of what is likely to happen in the course of interpretation over the centuries, but it is especially interesting because it takes narrative form.[31]

The same process may be observed in other characters, for instance Pilate, but of him I must speak more briefly. He was, of course, an historical character, of whom something is known from sources independent of the New Testament. He was Procurator of Judea from A.D. 26 to 36. According to Josephus he was a hard man, though, as C. K. Barrett observes, "he had successors whose little finger was thicker than his loins."[32] This historical character plays the role of Judge in our fable. As Betrayal needs a Betrayer, so Trial needs a Judge. And that is where his life in narrative interpretation begins. It continues in a very extraordinary fashion, for Pilate, though of course he was generally abominated, is already in the gospel accounts being given an unhistorical character, thoughtful, even compassionate; and he became a saint of the Coptic church. He met several different ends, including suicide and execution; and he also acquired a wife, who in her turn acquired a proper name.

In Mark's brief account, Pilate at the trial asks Jesus at once if he is King of the Jews, and gets, as I have said, a noncommittal reply; after that, nothing, despite the seriousness of the charges. Pilate wonders at this, then offers to release Jesus according to the (unhistorical) custom of the feast. Luke gives Pilate something more to say: "I find no crime in this man." John, at the second time of asking, repeats the *su legeis*, but so far from keeping a Marcan silence, uses the words as the introduction to a longish conversation: "You say I am a King. For this I was born," and so on. The conversation culminates in the famous question, "What is truth?" Pilate is now a thoughtful, philosophical figure; it was Bacon, in a later midrash, who said he was jesting, and did not stay for an answer. John's Pilate listens to a statement ("Everyone who is of the truth hears my voice") and asks a sensible question. He would still prefer to release Jesus. John's purpose here is first to establish that the aims of Jesus are not political, and secondly to whitewash Pilate and the Romans at the expense of the Jews. Crucifixion was a Roman penalty, freely awarded to militant revolutionaries; it was thus essential to explain that the situation was otherwise, and that the Jews had compelled Pilate to act.

When the Judge turns into a character, the development is much affected by these requirements, and he emerges as surprisingly considerate and sympathetic. Matthew provides him with a sensitive wife, and gives her a premonitory dream. He also invents the scene of Pilate washing his hands (quite implausible as history) and the saying "I am innocent of this man's blood; see to it yourselves," which leads on to the Jewish acceptance of guilt: "His blood be on our heads and on our children." This disastrous fiction has an Old Testament source in Deuteronomy 21:6–7 ("all the elders of the city nearest the slain man shall wash their hands ... and they shall testify, Our hands did not shed this blood"). Probably the words are also meant to recall Judas' blood-guilt. Anyway, the Judge acquired character. In Luke he is more judicial, and the matter of the extra hearing before Herod introduces a new political theme. In John he is a civilized debater; and it is John who gives him his most memorable sayings: "Behold the man," and, of the *titulus* for the cross, "What I have written I have written."

Here, then, are examples in plenty of what John Drury calls "midrashic development in historical writing." [33] Pilate is thoughtful, puzzled, a man who attends to the dreams of his wife; he is alert to political advantage, making a courteous or prudent gesture toward Herod;[34] he is moved by the mysterious power of his prisoner, and even discusses religion and ethics with him. Since we so rarely think of such characters as they occur in particular gospels, we have in our heads, when we think about Pilate, a mixture of all these qualities. The story went in search of a character, and more narrative followed, to explain the character further. There are many later fictions about Pilate. He persuades the emperor Tiberius of the divinity of Christ. He appears before Caesar wearing the seamless robe of Jesus (itself invented out of a testimony). When Caesar is about to cut off his head he prays that he be not destroyed along with the wicked Jews, and a voice from heaven declares that all generations and families of nations shall call him blessed — a midrash evidently founded on Luke's Magnificat, which is itself a midrash on Hannah's song in 1 Samuel 2.[35] The judicious men who established the canon tended to prefer documents with a more restricted application of the technique, but, as we have seen, it continued to flourish extra-canonically, and the manifest fictionality of the extra-canonical tradition no doubt strengthened, by contrast, the history-likeness of the canonical documents.

The matter of this chapter is really quite simple. Of an agent there is nothing to be said except that he performs a function: Betrayal, Judgment. When the agent becomes a kind of person, all is changed. It takes very little to make a character: a few indications of idiosyncrasy, of deviation from type, are enough, for our practiced eyes will make up the larger patterns of which such indications can be read as parts.

The key to all this development — from fable to written story, from story to character, from character to more story — is interpretation. At some point a narrative achieves a more or less fixed form; in the case of the gospels this was the formation of a more or less fixed canon. There were many other gospels, but their failure to achieve canonicity cost them their lives; four remain, and each illustrates in its own way the manner in which pre-canonical interpretation works. Some of the differences between them are no doubt due to the varying needs and interests of the communities for whom the evangelists originally wrote, and to their own diverse theological predispositions; but many are induced by the pressure of narrative interpretation, not independent of these other pressures, but quite different from the kinds of institutional commentary and exegesis that typically constitute post-canonical interpretation. For these early interpretations take the form of new narrative, whether by a reorganization of existing material or by the inclusion of new material. In the first stage this new material characteristically derives from texts — Old Testament texts — tacitly regarded as somehow part of the same story, the same universal plot of which the Passion is the denouement. But the new narrative itself generates character, and the characters generate new narrative beyond any immediate need, though the new narrative again takes its form from those more ancient texts in the first part of the book. It is only when the canon is closed that the work of interpretation becomes the work of exegesis,[36] and even that, as we know, can be pretty inventive. There is a genuine continuity between the operations performed on their material by the evangelists, and the work of the exegetes who, for almost two millennia, have continued their labors.

If we take all this into account, it will appear that what Henry James had to say about "the usual origin of the fictive picture" needs some amendment. He situates that origin at the point where agents begin to generate a story. Other, perhaps simpler, men, as he remarked, "see the fable first and make out its agents afterwards"; but then these agents hover and solicit, interest and appeal, as what they are — as reasonable simulacra of persons; and then begins the work of finding the right relations and complications consistent with one's measure of the truth. There, too, begin our interpretations, our inquiries into what stories originally meant and what they originally mean, so far as our perhaps delusive sense of their perhaps delusive radiance gives us warrant to speak.

V

What Precisely
Are the
Facts?

*If we write novels so, how
shall we write history?*
Henry James (on *Middlemarch*)

IF SO MANY causes act in concert to ensure that texts are from
the beginning and sometimes indeterminately studded with interpretations; and if these texts in their very nature demand
further interpretation and yet resist it, what should we expect
when the document in question denies its own opacity by
claiming to be a transparent account of the recognizable world?

In practice we may feel that we have no particular difficulty
in distinguishing between narratives which claim to be reliable
records of fact, and narratives which simply go through the
motions of being such a record. But when we think about it,
as on occasion we may compel ourselves to, the distinction
may grow troublesome. In this chapter I shall try to put myself
under that compulsion, and I shall do so by looking at the
Passion narratives as historical accounts. My approach, as it may
by this time be unnecessary to add, is that of a secular critic;
inquiries of this kind do of course have implications for Christian belief, but such implications have no relevance to the
present inquiry.

Here is a passage from John's gospel, as usual in the Revised
Standard Version: "Since it was the day of Preparation, in order
to prevent the bodies from remaining on the cross on the sabbath (for that sabbath was a high day), the Jews asked Pilate
that their legs might be broken, and that they might be taken
away. So the soldiers came and broke the legs of the first, and
of the other who had been crucified with him; but when they

came to Jesus and saw that he was already dead, they did not break his legs. But one of the soldiers pierced his side with a spear, and at once there came out blood and water. He who saw it has borne witness — his testimony is true, and he knows that he tells the truth — that you also may believe. For these things took place that the scripture might be fulfilled, 'Not a bone of him shall be broken.' And again another scripture says, 'They shall look on him whom they have pierced'" (John 19:31–37).

Only John has this part of the narrative. The first thing we notice about it, in all probability, is the strength of its claim to be a report of something that actually happened. This claim is asserted in several ways. Next day is not only the sabbath (which in itself could be represented as a reason for taking down the bodies, though in fact the Law ruled that they must be taken down before nightfall, sabbath or not) but Passover; John is reminding us of his chronology once more, but also, by emphasizing the peculiarity of the situation, achieving an effect of the real. Other confirmatory details work to the same end: soldiers were seen to break the legs of the other crucified men, but in the case of Jesus this happened not to be necessary, since he was dead already; nevertheless, one soldier was observed to pierce the side of Jesus with his spear. These events have an appearance of fortuity, they happened to occur, and the slight abnormalities of procedure reinforce the claim to factual reporting.

Moreover, the text demands urgently that we accept it as an eyewitness account. It seems that everything depends upon our doing so; hence the intervention in the narrative of a voice asserting its veracity. The Greek has a redundancy that bears the claim in on us: "the one who has seen has witnessed, and the witness of him is true, and he knows that he speaks truly." Nowhere else in the gospels, so far as I know, are we so insistently urged to accept a narrative as a transparent account of historical fact. Indeed, because it is so exceptional it has been thought to be spurious, an interpolation; but this view is not widely held.

The passage immediately following this intervention is

equally extraordinary, considered as part of a simple historical record. For it now appears that the intention of the report is not merely to provide an accurate and dependable account of what actually happened, to affirm as a matter of historical fact that the legs were not broken, that the dead man's side was pierced. It serves a further purpose: it affirms that these events had been foretold, in detail, a long time before. It claims that they were notable not merely because all the detail of so great an historical moment must be obviously so, but also because they were the fulfillment of discrete events in another, earlier narrative — events which if no such fulfillment had been recorded, could never have been supposed to need one, for they already had their own context in history and song. The soldier's failure to break the legs of Jesus, and the thrusting in of the spear, are therefore not only what is said to have happened, not only chronicle; they also continue and form part of an existing book, part of a literary plot. Indeed all historical explanation needs to establish between events relations that are not simply those of chronicle — using that word in something like Morton White's sense, to mean "a conjunction of non-causal singular statements which expressly mention [the] subject." [1] The transformation of non-causal chronicle into causal history, however it is done (and there are many different methods), is one reason why the disentangling of the concept of history from that of fiction is so much trickier than one might expect.

The Old Testament passages directly referred to by John seem to be a verse in Psalm 34, "He keeps all his bones; not one of them is broken," and another in Zechariah 12, "they look on him whom they have pierced." A deeper reference is to the rules given in a Septuagint version of Exodus 12:10 and in Numbers 9:12 for the slaughter of the Passover lambs, which is to be accomplished without the breaking of bones. As I said in the last chapter, John attached importance to the figurative relation of Jesus to the Passover lamb, the justification for which is probably yet another Old Testament text, Isaiah's messianic verse "he is brought as a lamb to the slaughter" (53:7). It was the existence of this text that gave figural force to the instructions for ritual slaughter, and then to the texts from Psalms and Zechariah, now drawn in to this subtextual network. Moreover, the blood and water that issued from the wound are not to be thought of as mere confirmatory detail, but as symbolic, presumably of Eucharist and Baptism, an interpretation still taken for granted in the hymn "Rock of Ages":

> Let the water and the blood
> From thy riven side which flowed
> Be of sin the double cure.

The origin of this symbolism is indicated by John 7:38: "as the scripture says, out of his belly shall flow streams of living water," the scripture quoted being uncertain.

So we have a catena of ancient texts, and some contemporary theological symbolism, brought into a fact-like narrative. Since this second, non-narrative microplot (if it may be so described), which lies latent in the historical record, has as its basis a typological relation between Jesus and the Passover sacrifice, we can say that it implies the larger typological relation, of the old dispensation to the new, the old rite to the new, and the old narrative to that of the end of time it covertly announced and foreshadowed.[2]

We now have before us a problem which so fascinated Erich Auerbach that he made it the center of his work. He greatly admired the realism of the gospels, and saw in them the origin of that *sermo humilis* which, over the centuries, was to be the bearer of later realism. But he knew also that the evangelists, and Christian interpreters for an exceedingly long time after them, were obsessed by typology, by *figura*, which is found, in the gospels, in easy coexistence with history-like narration.[3] The reconciliation of fact and *figura* is necessary not only here, but also in the Infancy narratives of Matthew and Luke, where the exertions of fiction on behalf of *figura* are rather more obvious; in the Passion narrative too great an emphasis on figural invention is likely still to scandalize. And some commentators continue to insist that the realism of John's narrative is easily explained: it conforms to the historical facts. The practice of breaking the legs of crucified criminals existed; it was an act of mercy, but Jesus was beyond the need of it. The verb translated "pierced" in verse 34 may rather mean "pricked" or "prodded," as if the soldier's object was the reasonable one of discovering whether Jesus was still alive.[4] On rare occasions blood and serum, which looks like water, may issue from a dead body. The verse about the veracity of the witness means exactly what it says. John provides an eyewitness account of the proceedings, and then passes on to suggest their deeper meanings by leading the reader to a consideration of types and symbols.

Such are the arguments of those who cannot accept that the historical account is an invention, founded on a repertory of texts brought to fulfillment by a literary narrative. Without adjudicating between the two positions, one may safely say that the passage strikingly combines what may be called reality-effects with an ability to comply with other literary texts. Nor is it unique in this; the discovery of recondite figurations in history-like narrative is a normal activity of secular criticism. By convention we tend to look for them not in narratives presented as having some transparence upon historical fact, but in fictions that reconcile a mimesis of reality with a more or less elaborate internal structure; but this distinction is more arbitrary than it seems, and figurations, usually of an ideological origin whether acknowledged or no, will be found in history as well as in the history-like. And anyway, if God writes the plot, the potential compatibility of narrative and *figura* is infinite.

I chose the example from John not because its method is unusual in this respect — on the contrary — but because the obtrusive insistence on its own historical reliability, though it only says what other examples imply, is out of the way; the literal truth of the report is as a rule more reticently affirmed. That affirmation is not made *in spite of* the fact that the narrative complies with Old Testament texts, for such compliance is clearly held to confirm the veracity of the narrative, to establish the fidelity of the historian to his chronicle. Yet the old texts have, at least in some cases, manifestly generated the new narrative.

Consider Psalm 22. It begins, "My God, my God, why hast thou forsaken me?" Then the poet complains that "all who see him jeer at him, make mouths and wag their heads, saying, 'He threw himself on the Lord for rescue; let the Lord deliver him, for he holds him dear.' They have pierced his hands and feet, shared out his garments among them, casting lots for his clothes." This single psalm is clearly a source, or, if you prefer, a prophecy or promise of incidents in the historical Passion narrative. The story fulfills the poem; the poem is, one might say, the kind of oracle I mentioned in my first chapter, a *klēdōn* — a pronouncement of which the meaning (though it may make sense in its own time) can be determined only much later, and by illumination from a context unpredicted and remote from that of the original utterance. There are various explanations as to how this oracle works. It may be a consequence of the divine homogeneity of God's world-plot; or it may happen because it is Jesus himself who speaks, in accurate figures, throughout the Old Testament.[5] Whatever the cause, we have a story written in such a way as to ensure pleromatic conformity with clues laid down in an earlier part of what was to be a single book. (I call the conformity pleromatic because, as I have said, the writers had a passion for fulfillment, fullness, completion, which are in Greek *plērōma*.) This is a distinctive operation; these plot relations are not of the causal kind admired and recommended by Aristotle. They are rather, to use the word in a special sense that has been current in recent years, "hermeneutic" — that is, the earlier texts are held to contain, possibly in a disguised or deceptive form, narrative promises that will later be kept, though perhaps in unexpected ways.

The habit of finding such clues was not confined to the evangelists, and the search continued after their narratives were established and canonized.[6] The same use of types and testimonies persisted: as proofs of divine organization, they were also proofs of the historicity of the narratives. It may seem to us that there is inherent in such practices the possibility that intertextual parallels may be forced or even faked; and there is evidence that the desire to "christologize" Old Testament texts could sometimes lead to their being rewritten in a more convenient form. A famous instance is the Christian version of Psalms 96:10, as found in Justin, where the words "from the tree" are added to the original text, "The Lord has reigned." [7] It is from the same Justin that we have a clear statement of the theory underlying this particular "hermeneutic" practice: "Sometimes . . . the Holy Spirit . . . has caused something to be done which was a type of what was to happen, sometimes He uttered words concerning what was to come about, phrasing them as if they referred to things taking place then or even having already taken place." [8] When both Testaments were available to scholars in codex form it was presumably easier to discover more instances, and so the "hermeneutic" process continued, as indeed it still does.[9]

So far as I know, this is a unique way of writing history. In its extreme form it implies the abolition of the Old Testament except in its role as a type-source for the New — in short, "the total destruction of its historical character." [10] The entire Jewish Bible was to be sacrificed to the validation of the historicity of the gospels; yet its whole authority was needed to establish that historicity. A mind habituated to modern assumptions about history may be inclined to see the emphasis on type and testimony as evidence that the narrative is fictitious; but on the view I am describing it is otherwise: the more farfetched and improbable the intertextual relations, the more certainly historical the narrative must be.

Let me now quote a historical, or pseudo-historical, narrative of a very different kind. It purports to describe an engagement between an American and a Russian warship off the coast of California: "What happened on the 9th March, 1864 . . . is not too clear. Popov the Russian admiral did send out a ship, either the corvette "Bogatir" or the clipper "Gaidamek," to see what it could see. Off the coast of either what is now Carmel-by-the-Sea, or what is now Pismo Beach, around noon or possibly toward dusk, the two ships sighted each other. One of them may have fired; if it did then the other responded; but both were out of range so neither showed a scar afterward to prove anything." [11] This passage describes an historical event which is held to have occurred, to have left no trace, and to be susceptible of honest report only in the most uncertain and indeterminate manner. It admirably represents a modern skepticism concerning the reference of texts to events. Events exist only as texts, already to that extent interpreted, and if we were able to discard the interpretative material and be as honest as historians, quite honestly, pretend to be, all we should have left would be some such nonsignificant dubiety as this account of the first engagement ever to take place between American and Russian forces. The book contains characters who attach importance to that encounter: members of a crackpot political party, and users of a communication system which bears no significant messages, and is in illegal opposition to the United States Post Office, which at least professes to do so. Their view of history exists only by the fiat of an absurd ideology. And as we read on the question arises, whether we do not live in a complex of semiotic systems which are either empty or are operated on the gratuitous assumption that a direct relation exists between a sign and a corresponding object "in reality." The only sense attributable to the naval engagement arises from the operation of coded fantasies in a lunatic group. And the impotence of that group, as we see from its account of the seafight, is such that their pseudo-history cannot supplant the official histories, which serve a different and much more successful ideology.

The story of the sea battle occurs not in the work of a professed historian, not even as a nightmare example in a book by some distracted philosopher of history, but in a novel called *The Crying of Lot 49*. It is, for all that, a serious historiographical exercise. It illustrates the point that we are capable of a skepticism very remote from the pleromatic certitudes of the evangelists, remote even from the sober historicism of only yesterday. We can, indeed, no longer assume that we have the capacity to make value-free statements about history, or suppose that there is some special dispensation whereby the signs that constitute an historical text have reference to events in the world. That it would not be possible to discover a passage like the one I have just quoted in a genuine historical work is an indication that we mostly go about our business as if the contrary of what we profess to believe were the truth; somehow, from somewhere, a privilege, an authority, descends upon our researches; and as long as we do things as they have generally been done — as long, that is, as the institution which guarantees our studies upholds the fictions that give them value — we shall continue to write historical narrative as if it were an altogether different matter from making fictions or, *a fortiori,* from telling lies.

Hence there is some difficulty in speaking of the interpretative fictions of the evangelists. On one side we are worried because to do so might seem a polite way of saying they lied (a most unhappy regression to the naive excesses of the Deists); and on the other because although we are aware that a particular view of the world, about what must or ought to happen, affects accounts of what does or did happen, we tend to repress this knowledge in writing and reading history, and allow it free play only when firmly situated on the differently privileged ground of fiction. Yet we have seen that literary forces of the kind that operate in fiction certainly affected the design of the gospel narrative. The recognition of such an influence entails consideration of the degree to which the chronicle is shaped into history by other extraneous forces which may be called theological or ideological, depending on where one stands; whatever we call them these forces must, insofar as they affect what is said and the manner of saying it, assume rhetorical forms. For example, it was important to the survival of the new religion that the evangelists' reports should be taken as true, against rival accounts. So they used all means to assert their truth; John's metanarrative voice is one such device, the provision of verisimilar detail is another. At the same time, it was necessary that the truth should be acceptable as such, that it should accord with contemporary presumptions as to what the truth was; and it was also necessary (though this is really part of the same point) that the report should have the backing of the scriptures.

The evangelists' way of writing history can perhaps best be observed at the crucial point of their narratives, the trial and execution. Their versions vary, perhaps because of access to different sources, perhaps because of progressive interpretation; but the combination of scriptural witness and "reality-effect" [12] is always impressive. All narrate the same series of events, and they were public events occurring at a fairly well specified historical moment, a moment probably within the lifetime of some of the original audience. We may ask two questions of these pieces of historical writing: how intimately are they related to Old Testament testimonies? How well do they conform with what may be plausibly said to have occurred? The answer to the first may be such as to suggest that parts of the narratives were generated from Old Testament texts, and are therefore interpretations of those texts, and so fictive. The answer to the second may suggest there is a difference between being able to make a text sound as if what it reports had occurred, and making it report what had occurred.

The first question may be briefly answered in this way (and the word "fulfill" may be taken as meaning "derive from"): The false witnesses at the Sanhedrin trial fulfill texts in Psalms 35 and 109; the silence of Jesus before his accusers fulfills Psalm 38 ("I behave like a man who cannot hear and whose tongue offers no defense," here assimilated to the "malicious witnesses . . . question me on matters of which I know nothing" of Psalm 35) and from the Suffering Servant passage in Isaiah 53 ("He was afflicted, he submitted to be struck down and did not open his mouth"). The spitting and buffeting are related to a whole cento of texts; the covering of the face has been traced to a misunderstanding of another Suffering Servant verse (53:3). Matthew omits it, Luke adds a bit of narrative to explain it. The blows of the servants fulfill Isaiah 50:6. As to the Crucifixion, Mark "contents itself with portraying the picture of the crucified in a few verses according to the 'Passion testimonies.' " [13] Mark has wine mingled with myrrh, from Proverbs 31; Matthew, reworking him, remembers Psalm 69 and substitutes gall for myrrh. The division of garments fulfills Psalm 22; the eclipse, the last words, the vinegar, and the death cry all have Old Testament sources.

This list could be much longer; the repertoire of narrative

germs was both extensive and extensible. According to Dodd,[14] Matthew used all Mark's testimonies except two, adding five of his own, including the silver of Judas and the raising of the dead at the time of the Crucifixion (which occurs in no other gospel, and is not a thing likely, as history, to have passed without general notice: Matthew is not really saying it happened, only that a line in Daniel suggested it should). Luke has four of Mark's and adds six of his own, including "Into your hands I commend my spirit," which is from Psalm 31, and replaces Mark's inarticulate cry. Of John's testimonies four coincide with Mark's and five do not, including the ones I mentioned earlier in this chapter. It is John's remark on the endlessness of the narrative possibilities that best expresses the Christian attitude to the testimonies: "if they [the deeds of Jesus] should be written every one, I suppose that even the world itself could not contain the books that should be written" (21:25).

We remind ourselves once again that these pleromatic conformities were intended not to detract from history-likeness, but on the contrary to enhance it. And for some modern scholars they continue to do so. Dodd, who had a highly developed sense of the ways in which a factual narrative could be constructed "according to the scriptures," nevertheless remarks that there were many more possible testimonies that could have been brought in and were not, and finds in this restraint a hint that the narratives do respect historical fact.[15] There is some desperation in this argument; for although there might seem to be practical limits to the number of Old Testament texts that could be used in this sense, there is no obvious way to define them strictly, as may be seen from Matthew's invention of the Judas narrative; and given the extent of the possibilities, how shall we say that this or that narrative fails to exploit them as fully as it would have done had that been one of its important aims? Dodd's point could be made with the same force, or lack of it, if there were twice as many allusions to testimonies in the accounts.

It must appear, then, that the historical record as we have it is constructed in considerable measure from the testimonies, in a manner now sufficiently familiar. And we come to the second question, the matter of plausibility. That these accounts have seemed plausible and continue to do so is not the point; for to seem plausible is the aim of a great deal of fiction. The trial has been the subject of minute inquiry and endless dispute; moreover, the four accounts of it vary, sometimes incompatibly.[16] Many scholars accept that there could not have been a night trial before the Sanhedrin; that although it is true that capital sentences had to be confirmed the following morning, this could not be done on a feast day; that no accusation of blasphemy could have succeeded on the evidence; that even if it had, the penalty would have been stoning and the matter would not have gone before the Roman governor.[17] Pilate's behavior at the Roman hearing is nowhere credible. It is most improbable that there could have been an event corresponding to the release of Barabbas; that story may arise from an ideological need to distinguish Jesus from the Zealots and freedom-fighters of the period, or from the motif of mock-worship variously inserted into the narratives and conceivably connected with a ritual in which the mock-king was called kerabas.[18]

It is fairly widely agreed that an original narrative less acceptable to the ideologies of the writer-interpreters has been covered over in their accounts of the trials. With different emphases it is argued that the political interests of Jesus must have been stronger than now emerges; that he was a Zealot, and so, like Barabbas, a lēstēs (not really "thief" so much as "terrorist" or "revolutionary"). His trial before Pilate would then have been on a charge of sedition; this was of course unacceptable to the church; and since the sentence of crucifixion, which was the usual Roman punishment for sedition, could hardly be written out of the record, there had to be a narrative explaining that the Jews forced this inappropriate trial and sentence on the reluctant Pilate. And by the time these documents were written, the need to attribute guilt for the death of Jesus to the Jews rather than the Romans had increased.[19]

Yet whatever the necessary distortions, the narrative must continue to seem factual, for, as C. F. D. Moule puts it, the faith "stood or fell with the sober facts of the story."[20] Here was a strong incitement to "realism"; and a remarkable degree of realism was achieved, despite the competing demands of the figural plot, and the necessities of ideology. The gospels sound like history, and that they do so is the consequence of an extraordinary rhetorical feat, one without which the Resurrection would not have had its place in a context of sober fact. Everybody notices how different the Passion narratives are from what precedes them; they have a quality not to be found in their prologues. The opening chapters are seemingly incoherent, generically uncertain; clues as to their progression, climax, and closure must be sought with a charitable interpretative eye. Such orders as are found in them are hardly *narrative* orders. We do not remember them in order as they are written, or not without a special effort. They lack the great mnemonic, plot — the fulfillment of narrative promise, the insistence on cause and regulated sequence, and harmonious interrelation between what has gone before and what is now being said.

Nor is it merely that we are more likely to remember a plotted narrative; we are also less likely to ask awkward questions about it. This is why historians as well as novelists (traditionally) place such value on "followability"; it limits the possibility of awkward questions, it leaves less to explain; for historians usually write narrative rather than explanation if they can. Thus the detection of occult figurations, and the questioning of the narrative as a report on fact, is delayed.

The delay was lengthened, in the present instance, by the power of the institution which undertook to uphold the absolute veracity of the reports, and to enforce it not only by dogma but by the use of vast resources of liturgy, sacrament, and art. We should never underestimate our predisposition to believe whatever is presented under the guise of an authoritative report and is also consistent with the mythological structure of a society from which we derive comfort, and which it may be uncomfortable to dispute. This desire for comfort, this willingness to believe what bears the ordinary signs of the credible, explains the rhetorical success of such works as Defoe's "Apparition of Mrs. Veal." There is an agreed way of registering reality; and it has authority over us. There is also authority in the person making the report or maintaining its veracity; part, but not all, of this is the mere authority of the printed word. There is also the authority of the institution or the person.

Everybody knows that Sir Philip Sidney, dying on the field of Zutphen, gave up his drink of water to a wounded soldier, saying, "Thy necessity is greater than mine." The story was first told by Sidney's friend Fulke Greville, in a biography written twenty-five years after the poet's death, and first published forty years after that. We know from what he says of Sidney's own writings that Greville approved of characters in books only when their conduct might serve as an example to the reader; and he presented Sidney as a model of virtue. There were no surviving eyewitnesses to his dying act, for which we have only Greville's word; and it has been pointed out that Greville seems to have been remembering a passage in Plutarch's *Life of Alexander*.[21] Whether it happened or not, the offer of the drink is what ideally ought to have happened. Too strict a distinction between meaning and truth would leave few historical narratives capable of interesting us; it is necessary to remember, as Spinoza remarked, that they are written by human beings.

WE HAVE SEEN some of the ways in which this history-like writing must depart from and distort the chronicle. There is another way, which I have mentioned and must now mention again. It is not peculiar to gospel history, but that it is effective in gospel history I tried to show when talking about John's version of the Leavetaking. It is, simply enough, the literary organization involved in elaborating a fable. Consider Mark's story of Peter's denial, which Jesus prophesied after he had prophesied his betrayal. Mark inserts the story of Peter in the courtyard within the account of the first Sanhedrin trial. The effect is to make the disciple's denial and the master's sole public claim to messiahship as nearly simultaneous as narrative allows. Noticing this, conventional scholarship tends to call it "homiletic." The episode is exemplary: under persecution behave like Jesus, not like Peter. But there is more to be said of this, and of Mark's other "analepses."[22] We tend not to give them the kind of attention we would think appropriate to the interpolated sequences of an epyllion, whether Alexandrian or in the imitations of Catullus or the Elizabethan erotic poets. There we see an invitation to interpret; here the word "homiletic" dismisses the case.

Or, to take a more familiar example, how much interpretation has been granted to the Comices scene in *Madame Bovary*! While M. Lieuvain and M. Derozeray orate to the crowd about freedom, order, and duty, Emma and Rodolphe make love; both lovemaking and oration are punctuated by shouts about sheep, pigs, and manure; and the episode ends when Catherine Leroux is rewarded for a lifetime of servitude by a gift of twenty-five francs, which she will give to the priest for masses. We can hardly wait to begin. This famous passage is certainly more complex than Mark's, but it does share with the gospel some structural principles, notably the insertion of two narratives into the same rendering of a temporal continuum. Flaubert might have done more with Mark's idea, cutting back and forth, interspersing the cockcrows into the dialogue of the trial; but Mark does the main work, bringing together the "I am" of Jesus, his sole, brilliantly lit assertion — so unexpected that some early texts changed it to the usual noncommittal "You have said so" — and the denial of the chief and representative disciple. After that achievement the rest is only detail; John provides some, explaining how Peter got into the High Priest's courtyard in the first place, telling us that one of Peter's interlocutors was a kinsman of the servant whose ear had recently been cut off. But Mark's interest is in the space between two concurrent events. Luke abolishes that space for the sake of a moving recognition: his Jesus turns and looks upon Peter (22:61). That closes the matter; Mark does not close matters so readily. Considered diegetically, narrowly, as part of the narrative of Jesus' trial, his denial scene is null; it is for interpretation to fill the gap, to conflate denial and affirmation; to relate it to the betrayal of Judas and the flight of the other disciples; to reflect that this is the last we ever see, in the second gospel, of Peter, Matthew's rock. In Mark he blunders into mystery; his prime recognition of the Messiah, right in the middle of the book, is at once marred by his caring for the things of man

tors, but their presence in an historical account gives it a different generic feel — it becomes a memoir. The advantage of third-person narration is that it is the mode which best produces the illusion of pure reference.[24] But it *is* an illusion, the effect of a rhetorical device. We cannot escape the conclusion that "the fact can exist only linguistically, as a term in a discourse," although "we behave as if it were a simple reproduction of something or other on another plane of existence altogether, some extra-structural 'reality'." [25]

An understanding of this, and of the dependence we have on the myth that felicitous assertion equals accurate reference, has occasionally led writers of narrative to tease us out of our delusion by "foregrounding" the differences between real and narrative time, and by destroying our illusions of narrative causality and closure. Sterne did it at the beginning of the novel, before the conventions had time to be confused with the truth; and lately it has become a dominant mode of serious narrative. Not for nothing is the purpose of the *nouveau roman* said to be "disappointment" (*déception*), and not for nothing does it wage its campaign against vulgar mimesis. We resist, drugged by the comfort of the conventional, fearing the consequences of losing an accessible truth.[26]

Historians are aware of these problems, but tend to confine discussion of them to a separate discipline called "philosophy of history." Within that enclosure they discuss, each in his own way, the relation between history and chronicle. Few, I think, maintain, when thinking along these lines, that there can be an immediate relation between history-writing and "what actually happened" (*wie es eigentlich gewesen*, in Ranke's famous formula). Indeed they seem to be most interested in questions of explanation and narrative, that is, in matters of telling and causal connection (explanations are ways of filling gaps in the causal sequence established by the narrative, a kind of modern midrash). They think that history, like story, has to have the property of "followability," to use W. B. Gallie's word;[27] that a history — in Arthur Danto's phrase — is "a narrative structure imposed upon events." [28] Such narratives will have the logical structure of other stories, though their purpose is to provide explanations by establishing connections other than those immediately suggested by a chronicle sequence.

This philosophical effort seems to be directed at the same problems that I have been discussing in relation to the Passion narratives. We are offered a narrative structure, with all its mnemonic and suasive advantages. We get the benefits of followability, and whatever is followable is on the way to being acceptable. A "convincing" narrative convinces mainly because it is well-formed and followable, though for other reasons also; for instance, it reassures us by providing what appears to be an impartially accurate rendering of reality. When John gives the distance from Bethany to Jerusalem, and names the place where Pilate sat in judgment, he may well be wrong in both cases, but the detail is immediately reassuring.

Gallie observes that following a story is "a teleologically guided form of attention." [29] And as many others have argued, to make arrangements for such guidance is to have some ulterior motive, whether it is aesthetic, epistemological, or ethical (which includes "ideological"). These are Morton White's categories of metahistorical control or motive; others have more complex schemes.[30] According to William James, "the preferences of sentient creatures are what *create* the importance of topics";[31] and Nietzsche, in "The Use and Abuse of History," declared that "for a fact to exist we must first introduce meaning." All this we know, even if we behave as if we did not. The historical narrative comes to us heavily censored (as the account of a dream is censored) but also heavily interpreted (as that same account is affected by the dogmatic presuppositions of the analyst, which are, as Habermas says, "translated into the narrative interpretation.") [32] The historian cannot write, nor can we read, without prejudice. I hope we have seen that this is true of the gospel narratives.

Such a view of history-writing, suitably refined for philosophers and semiologists, might be generally acceptable; but once more we have to remember how difficult it is to behave as if it were correct. We are so habituated to the myth of transparency that we continue, as Jean Starobinski neatly puts it, to ignore *what is written* in favor of *what it is written about.*[33] One purpose of this book is to reverse that priority, which is why I am at the moment peculiarly conscious of the difficulty of doing so. And indeed the story of modern biblical exegesis (another history, with its own provision of prejudices) seems to confirm the view that it takes a powerful mind to attend to what is written at the expense of what it is written about.

The scholarly tradition that cultivated seriously this form of attention was the Jewish; and from our point of view its most influential representative was Spinoza. When he drew up his rules of scriptural interpretation in the seventh chapter of the *Tractatus Theologico-Politicus* he distinguished strictly between meaning and truth (what is written and what it is written about): in exegesis "we are at work," he said, "not on the truth of passages but on their meaning." And he expressed a particular dislike for the practice of distorting meaning "in order to make it conform with some truth already entertained." He neatly convicts his illustrious predecessor Maimonides of this offense, which he thinks intellectually disreputable and liable to favor political authoritarianism. The Bible, he held, "leaves reason absolutely free"; it is of divine origin, but it is accommodated to human understanding, which may ascertain its meanings, but must not confound them with truths. "It is one thing to understand the meaning of Scripture, and quite another to understand the actual truth." [34] Five centuries of Jewish interpretative rationalism stood behind Spinoza; but he was addressing the problems of his own day, and saw that the confusion of meaning and truth might result in the suppression of religious liberty. His pious book seemed blasphemous in 1670; so powerful is the atavistic preference for truth over meaning.

It was through the English Deists, some of whom were with better cause thought shocking, that Spinoza influenced the European tradition of biblical scholarship from the late eighteenth century on. A hundred years after Spinoza, Johann Michaelis could state that there was no reason to think the evangelists inspired in their account of history; and Lessing argued that "if no historical truth can be demonstrated, then nothing can be demonstrated by means of historical truths." Kant calmly dismissed the argument about history as irrelevant: "why should we entangle ourselves in such terribly learned investigations and disputes over an historical narrative, which we should always have left where it belonged, (among the *adiaphora* [matters of indifference]) when it is with *religion* that we have to do?" And so on, to David Friedrich Strauss.

This early firmness of tone was not maintained. It was, perhaps, not easy for German scholars to shut out the echoes of Luther's voice, which had laid it down that when a text is literal rather than manifestly allegorical, and when it is also narrative, then it must be historical.[35] The consequences of this conflict are the subject of a subtle and interesting book by Hans W. Frei. One of them was the development of modern hermeneutics. The distinction between meaning and truth in the biblical narratives — whether one accepted it or denied it — required new principles of interpretation. Among the new concepts this need engendered was "history-likeness" (*Geschichtsähnlichkeit*); it was necessary to disentangle this quality from guaranteed truth.

Frei describes the evolution of various hermeneutics intended to allow for the existence of such necessary distinctions without requiring the sacrifice of everything the practitioner held dear. An example is Herder's argument that history can mean "the kind of consciousness represented by a specific kind of account . . . To be historical . . . an account need not be of any specific occurrence that had actually taken place." Herder also said that "whoever turns a gospel of Christ into a novel has wounded my heart."[36] What he needed was the right to affirm the factual truth of scripture without having to decide whether its meaning lay in its having happened or merely in its having been written. Noting a similar compromise in Strauss, Frei explains these confusions of factuality with fact-likeness by saying that the Germans, unlike the English, had small experience of nonhistorical realistic narrative (they got the Higher Criticism but we got the Novel).[37] So the notion that the story *was* the meaning lay beyond their grasp. This is ingenious but questionable. But of the confusion between history-likeness and history there is no doubt; we still suffer from it, though later criticism reduced the historical Jesus to a shadow, and the interpretative and metahistorical motives of the evangelists have been minutely examined. The claim that the gospels are truth-centered continues for many to entail the proposition that they are in some sense factual, even though the claim takes the form of saying that the fact they refer to is a theology. It remains exceedingly difficult to treat them as stories, as texts totally lacking transparency on event.

And of course it is true that John's account of the breaking of the legs and the spear thrust, or Mark's account of Peter's denial, could hardly have achieved such success in the world had they been recorded in the manner of Pynchon's naval battle. The evangelists too were writing for a small community regarded as eccentric and possessing a communication system at odds with that of officialdom, but their object was different. It would have seemed insane to the author of John's gospel to profess not to know which ship was sent out, or where the sighting occurred, or whether either ship fired; or to allow that there was no physical evidence to prove that the encounter took place. And it would have seemed equally insane to believe that the world was a mass of interlinked communication systems bearing no messages, or only messages of the utmost triviality. He may have thought of the world as like a book; but if so the system was saturated with messages of the very highest importance. Lest they should be disbelieved or misunderstood or corrupted, there was a need for realism, and an equal need for the structure of *testimonia*, so that this sequence of events should seem a piece of, even the crown of, an historical development perceptible to the eye of the interpreter and written into the structure of the world, now seen as a book, as a codex. So it continued to be seen, by Dante at the climax of his poem, by Mallarmé at the end of the great age of the book. Pynchon's joke belongs to another age, which we have still hardly come to terms with.

The novel simulated the authority conferred on history by this perfect match of book and world. Henry James, the great master of research into the formal possibilities of fiction, con-

tinued to regard history-likeness as one of its essential characteristics. He thought the novelist was obliged to maintain the
fiction that his fiction is history, and expostulated against Trol-
lope for his carelessness in keeping up such appearances. It may
be, as Hillis Miller argues,[38] that the maintenance of such fictions, and especially of the fiction that a narrative text may be
transparent on fact, requires the acceptance of a culture that
imposes its own conditions, including its unexamined teleolo-
gies and its sense of endings, and that even in the nineteenth
century there were signs that these beliefs and assumptions
were being "demythologized." He finds attempts at demytholo-
gizing in *Middlemarch*. There may be stirrings in George Eliot
of a new attitude to meaning in history (she knew Strauss, of
course, as well as Charles Lyell and Darwin) but she had by
no means lost the desire to report everything aright, *wie es
eigentlich gewesen*, as her notebooks tell us clearly enough.
What precisely are the facts? It is a very George-Eliotish question: what are the facts about the first cholera epidemic, or the
1832 Reform Act, or the laws of inheritance, or German biblical
scholarship, or whatever came up and had to be consistent with
history-likeness. No doubt she would have said that in reading
her novels one ought to be working on meaning rather than
truth (she greatly admired Spinoza) but the novels still exploit
the cultural identification of the two. Nor are we, and the
modern historians, so at home in a new age that we do not, for
the most part, continue to countenance the benign deceit. How
far we do so because of the saturation of our culture by the gospels and traditional interpretations one need not try to say.

   All modern interpretation that is not merely an attempt at
"re-cognition" involves some effort to divorce meaning and
truth. This accounts for both the splendors and the miseries
of the art. Insofar as we can treat a text as not referring to what
is outside or beyond it, we more easily understand that it has
internal relationships independent of the coding procedures by
which we may find it transparent upon a known world. We
see why it has latent mysteries, intermittent radiances. But in
acquiring this privilege, the interpreters lose the possibility of
consensus, and of access to a single truth at the heart of the

thing. No one, however special his point of vantage, can get past all those doorkeepers into the shrine of the single sense. I make an allegory, once more, of Kafka's parable; but some such position is the starting point of all modern hermeneutics except those which are consciously reactionary. The pleasures of interpretation are henceforth linked to loss and disappointment, so that most of us will find the task too hard, or simply repugnant; and then, abandoning meaning, we slip back into the old comfortable fictions of transparency, the single sense, the truth.

VI

The
Unfollowable
World

*I marvel at how this great wealth
has made its home in this poverty.*
Gospel according to Thomas

I HAVE BEEN considering, under different aspects, some of the
forces that make interpretation necessary and virtually impossible, and some of the constraints under which it is carried on.
I have spoken of deafness and forgetfulness as properties not
only of texts, but of history, and of interpreters; of the pre-
emption of sense by institutions and by theoretical presuppositions; of our readiness to submit the show of things to the desires of our minds; of the structures of explanation which come
between us and the text or the facts like some wall of wavy
glass. And I have suggested that interpretation, which corrupts
or transforms, begins so early in the development of narrative
texts that the recovery of the real right original thing is an
illusory quest. Yet we continue to distinguish those within,
who know the truth before the parable breaks in and corrupts
it, and those without, to whom it is not given to do so. For the
former there is nothing in the stories but the appearance of
explanations; they look like *hoti*, but they are truly *hina*. Yet
to them also the stories are opaque. They may be content that
narratives which have the air of open proclamations are in fact
obscurely oracular; but in the end they too are prevented from
making definitive interpretations.

Much of what I have said will be disallowed by defenders of
a hermeneutics more conservative than mine, and, doubtless
with scorn, by a flourishing radical party, which would not

admit that its investigations are properly to be called hermeneutic, and which despises the very word "interpretation." Yet we are all, on a broad enough view, concerned with the same problem. Some suppose that it is right to inquire strictly into the question of what the text originally meant. Others wish to discover what it originally means, a more charismatic quest. Some seek to liberate texts from all historical constraint by a process of "deconstruction," others speak of foregoing the banal pleasures of continuity with the original sense for the sake of a joy more acute, if more dismaying, a *jouissance* that goes beyond the pleasure principle and arises from a quasi-sexual experience of loss and perversity. Yet all practice divination, however intermittently, erroneously, dishonestly, or disappointedly; most of all, disappointedly. For whether one thinks that one's purpose is to re-cognize the original meaning, or to fall headlong into a text that is a treacherous network rather than a continuous and systematic sequence, one may be sure of one thing, and that is disappointment. It has sometimes been thought, and in my opinion rightly, that the world is also like that; or that we are like that in respect of the world. Yet we have ways of working through the world, and ways of explaining unfollowable texts. There are certain conditions which make the task more comfortable: more or less acquiescent in the authority of institutions, more or less happy that we have an acquired taste for fulfillments, for a state of affairs in which everything hangs together, we accept a measure of private intermittency in our interpretations — unless we are unhappy because such acquiescence is an acceptance of untruth, and prefer antinomianism and the unhappiness of an even more complete isolation. In any case, a sense of mystery is a different thing from an ability to interpret it, and the largest consolation is that without interpretation there would be no mystery. What must not be looked for is some obvious public success. To see, even to perceive, to hear, even to understand, is not the same thing as to explain or even the same thing as to have access. The desires of interpreters are good because without them the world and the text are tacitly declared to be impossible; perhaps they are, but we must live as if the case were otherwise.

IN CHAPTER FIVE I offered — as a simple instance of necessary interpretative supplement — some comments on the narrative of Peter's Denial. It is one of those intercalations or analeptic narrative constructions of which Mark was so fond; and it is by no means the most difficult of them. In this chapter I shall move toward what may be a cheerless conclusion by saying more about the Marcan use of this device. Hope is a symptom of the interpreter's disease, as it is of terminal tuberculosis — the *spes hermeneutica* as I have called it — and I have some hope that by a consideration of the parts of the narrative in which Mark complicates the fable by intercalation we may come to learn something of the whole gospel. Perhaps (the disease begins to rage) there is a secret at the heart of Mark which is not a theology and perhaps not even really a secret; but rather some habit of narrative paradox or conjunction that might, in the end, be best represented without the use of words, in a diagram or by algebra. Strictly formalized, intercalation might be the clue to the whole, from the small part under consideration to the entire gospel as it stands in the larger book, intercalated between the long past (the beginning of which it boldly recapitulates in its first word, *archē*, the beginning) and the imminent ending.

But in following that line we may discover that, as usual, we have dropped into a duller subject, and are speaking rather of ourselves than of the book, since we cannot avoid the reflection that we ourselves are intercalated into the story in precisely this way, between the long past (which we recapitulate) and the imminent ending, which is our own, and, like Mark's, no parousia but a matter of fear and silence. Augustine, who did a good deal of thinking about the world under the form of the book, advised his flock to reflect, when they read Mark on the end of all things ("of that day or that hour no one knows," 13:32), on their own last day.[1] And indeed apocalypse, which is the genre Mark adapts in his thirteenth chapter, is the great literary vehicle of the moment of epochal transition, the period that is interposed between the past and the imminent end. Mark places his own "little apocalypse" in the space between his account of the ministry and his account of the Passion. It is the largest of his intercalations, in fact, an analepsis that is certainly homodiegetic, an incursion of the future, properly terrible, properly ambiguous, into a narrative which proleptically shapes and sanctifies it.

Mark is a brief gospel, but it contains at least nine instances of the procedure I am talking about.[2] His predilection has not passed without notice, but it is not often taken seriously. Though an evident idiosyncracy of Mark's narrative style it is rarely adduced as evidence that one is dealing with sophisticated storytelling, for on other grounds that seems not to be an attribute of Mark; and the intercalations are usually mentioned only to be explained away, for example by an hypothesis of double origin, or of intrusion by some later redactor,[3] or of an attempt by Mark to change the story in the service of "dogmatic and pragmatic ends."[4] Sometimes, when conscience suggests that it is not enough to explain *away*, a commentator may refer in passing to the literary force of these doubled narratives. For example, the interpolated account of the death of John the Baptist (6:14–29) has been praised for its unusual (un-Marcan) refinement,[5] and compared with the famous flashback in *Odyssey* xix, where, into the story of how Euryclea recognized Odysseus, there is interpolated a long narrative of the boar hunt at which, many years earlier, the hero got his telltale scar. Auerbach has an essay on this passage, celebrating its fullness and simplicity, and making much of its difference from the story of the sacrifice of Isaac; it simply seemed worth telling how Odysseus got the scar, and expounding the long-past event in accordance with its own interest, and at its own length.[6] But Mark's flashback, telling of Herod's fairytale promise to Salome, of her dance, and of her asking, at the prompting of her mother, for the Baptist's head, is not obviously prompted by some crucial moment (for example, of recognition) in the principal narrative, and it has nothing of that Homeric relaxation.

At 6:12 Jesus sends the Twelve off on a mission. They return, and make their report, at 6:30. In between comes the Salome story. Herod, we are told, is of the opinion that Jesus is John the Baptist risen from the dead; others take him to be

Elijah, or a prophet. We have not yet been told of John's death; so it is explained that Herod had imprisoned him to please his wife, Herodias, who held a grudge against John for saying that her marriage to Herod was unlawful. Herod, for his own part, finds John interesting; and it is only because he cannot break his promise — to give his stepdaughter practically anything she asks for — that he grants her what she demands, the head of John on a platter. Having got it, she gives it to her mother. The disciples of John then take his body and lay it in a tomb. At this point the disciples of Jesus return from their mission.

Here, then, is a genuine example of what a modern narrative analyst, following Genette, might call heterodiegetic analepsis. It is also "completive," because we already know of John's ministry and his arrest; thus this intrusion of a different story into the narrative flow of the story of Jesus completes an account of the Baptist's career. But although the episode belongs to that other story, and is thus properly called "heterodiegetic," it is close kin to the principal narrative. The ministry of Jesus began at the moment when John was taken; perhaps it began because he was taken.[7] Moreover Herod holds strongly to the view that Jesus is a reincarnation or double of John, so the intrusion of this completive account of John's life, at an early stage of Jesus' life, is a kind of prolepsis. And we may remember that John's disciples took his body and laid it in a tomb when we get to the end of the principal narrative and discover that Jesus' disciples did nothing of the sort; they ran away and left the task to Joseph of Arimathea.

At any rate, it seems harmless to say that this story of John and his disciples, cut into the narrative of Jesus and his disciples, was intended to complicate the master narrative by disrupting it, or by reflecting it in a partially distorted mirror. We can speculate as to the full character of that intention, for example, by considering the whole history of Jesus' relation with John as we know it from the not wholly compatible versions given by Josephus and by the fourth gospel; and so we may find "dogmatic and pragmatic" motives. But when such questions as to intention have been answered as well as they can be, we are, if we concern ourselves with meaning and not with truth, still to begin the task of interpretation. Here is an intrusive story, not essential to the principal fable, yet lying so close to it that its similarities of theme and dissimilarities of tone cannot help affecting it. It tells of an improbable dance by a little girl (*korasion*) and her monstrous request, conveyed through her by her cruel and sexually depraved mother. Both the dance and the request are grossly inappropriate to Salome's prepuberty, for both are strongly and perversely sexual. We need not look far for evidence that this is a situation inviting imaginative midrash. There is all the folklore of the daughters of Herodias, and the proliferating interpretations of the story by great artists: Flaubert, Mallarmé, Wilde, Yeats, Richard Strauss, to say nothing of the more curious fantasies of lesser writers, one of whom has Salome clutching the severed head between her thighs. The possibilities for interpretation are probably endless, even if we take the story of Salome as a unit in itself. We should still not have begun the work of describing the effects produced by its intrusion into another story, in which a master sends away his disciples to cure and exorcise, to rid people of unclean spirits. Salome is possessed by one, Herod is trapped into a kind of incest, Herodias demands a symbolic castration; of all this uncleanness John is the victim.

A favorite explanation of commentators not content to let the whole thing pass as a clumsiness or a fortuity is that the episode was put in to fill the gap between the departure of the Twelve and their return.[8] This, I'm afraid, gives one an insight into the remarkable naiveté of professional exegesis when confronted with problems of narrative; behind it, perhaps, is a lingering obsession with historicity, a wish to go on thinking of the gospel narrative as a map of truth. When, in sober fact, time passed, time must pass in the story. But stories are rarely like that, and Mark's story is very plainly not like that. His having disturbed the narrative line in this way makes the better commentators a bit uneasy; this passage, they may say, stands on "a somewhat higher cultural level than is normal for Mark."[9] So they seek evidence that it is not his. For example, Mark is usually over-fond of the historic present, but this trait is absent from the Salome narrative. Yes, but this is a temporally recessed interlude, and the avoidance of the historic present may mean no more than that the text exhibits a measure of narrative tact. Or: words are used here that are used nowhere else in Mark. True, but where else did he describe a girl dancing before a tipsy king? It is hard to avoid the conclusion that the commentators are swayed, perhaps unconsciously, by a desire to save their text from its own complexity, if only because that complexity draws attention to its distance from simple chronicle, and asserts the Spinozan distinction between meaning and truth.[10]

Another example of intercalation is the story of the woman with the hemorrhage, which is dovetailed into the story of the raising of Jairus' daughter (5:21–43) — the only instance of two miracle-stories being conflated in this way. To avoid falling into the habit of treating the gospel as a series of originally independent episodes loosely cobbled together, it might be wise to look at this twinned narrative in a fuller context. It is preceded by the story of the cure of the Gerasene demoniac, for which Jesus had crossed over to the other side of the lake, Gentile territory (they kept pigs there). After the cure he sails back across the lake and, disembarking, is immediately surrounded by a great crowd. Now Jairus arrives, a ruler of the synagogue, and asks Jesus to cure his sick daughter. Jesus goes with him, the crowd following. Into this throng there steals a sick woman; she has "had a flow of blood for twelve years" and has "suffered much under many physicians." She secretly touches Jesus' robe, and is at once conscious of having been healed. Jesus feels that power has gone out of him, and asks: Who touched my clothes? (The disciples, with their usual dullness, regard this as an absurd question to ask in such a crowd; Matthew omits their reaction, and indeed omits the crowd; 9:18–26.) There follows recognition between Jesus and the woman, and he sends her away healthy. Now comes the news that the daughter of Jairus is dead. Jesus nevertheless persists in going to her, shedding the crowd as he does so, but taking the parents with him. As he approaches he announces that the girl is only sleeping, and is laughed at for saying so. He takes the girl's hand, utters an Aramaic incantation, and tells her to rise. She does so. He commands them (the parents?) to silence, tells them to give her something to eat, and departs.

Why is the story of the sick woman intruded into that of the child? One common answer is, because it happened like that. Taylor's standard commentary takes this line; but then Taylor can seriously state that "the intercalation of narratives is not a feature of Mark's method." [11] As in only a few other places Mark here finds more to say than Matthew or Luke; he has a quite unusual amount of detail, which the others abbreviate, perhaps thinking Mark gave the incident undue prominence. Mark alone gives the age of the girl: she is twelve. The woman has been sick for twelve years; but this chiming can be, and is, dismissed as a coincidence, especially since "twelve" may mean no more than "quite a few." Yet in matters of this kind there is really no such thing as nonsignificant coincidence, and we are entitled to consider that this coincidence signifies a narrative relation of some kind between the woman and the girl.

So: an older woman is cured of a menstrual disorder of twelve years' standing, and is sent back healthy, no longer ritually unclean, into society. A girl who has not yet reached puberty is as it were reborn. (Mark alone of the synoptics refrains from saying she was dead; at the end he simply says the girl "stood up." Matthew alters the verb to improve the sense of resurrection. Indeed Matthew is clear what kind of story this ought to be: it is about bringing a child back to life. Mark, as usual, prefers the shadows. The restoration of the girl is greeted with expressions of amazement unusual even for Mark, who specializes in them; but they are not to be explained by saying the girl was raised from the dead. He keeps as many options open as possible.) The girl, once up and about, is perfectly normal, and needs food.[12] She too is welcomed back into society, no longer unclean.

When Jesus approaches her supposed corpse she is called "the child," but in healing her he addresses her as "little girl" (korasion, the same word used of Salome). The word is still a neuter, but it can only mean "little girl"; the change distinguishes her as approaching, from the other side, the condition of the cured woman, a healthy sexual maturity. The name

"Jairus" (missing from some manuscripts) is said to mean "the awakener," and it occurs in the book of Esther, which Mark knew well, and on which he drew in the Salome episode. Esther contains the story of a beautiful girl who survives the danger of death by inducing a sleepless king to touch her with a golden scepter. Is the story of the little girl a transformation of that story? We may reflect that when the hemorrhaging woman touches Jesus' garment what goes out of him is called "power," *dunamis*, a word with a great range of senses in Greek, including sexual senses, rather as the word "virtue" — another possible translation — does, or did until recently, in English.

I must not make too much of this, and anyway my task is not so much to offer interpretations as to speak of their modes, their possibilities, and their disappointments. My point is absolutely not that Mark is here "saying something" about sexuality; only that by looking at the twinned narratives in this way we might see how a text can as it were cultivate structural oppositions, bring together significantly antithetical persons or actions or even words. This text seems to be continually interested in providing instances of a generalized opposition between clean and unclean, and we ought not to dispose of this fact by some historical discourse about Jewish Law. The woman, in the present instance, is ritually unclean so long as her hemorrhage continues; but she is at once, by an exercise of power, *dunamis*, relieved of this disability. The girl, dead or supposed dead, is also unclean, or supposed unclean; she is restored by an exercise of power which is, in antithetical contrast, explicit and willed. Between the opposites clean and unclean there are inserted — intercalated — figures of sexual or magical force. We can safely say that these stories do not have the same meanings we should have found in them had they been told *seriatim*.

The practice is so often repeated as to become part of the habit of the book; and this repetition makes one wonder whether the intercalated stories do not exist to replicate, in particular episodes, some feature characteristic of the whole discourse. Should we think of the whole gospel as an intercalated story? It is inserted between another story and its end. It divides and joins the promises and the fulfillments. It is an insertion, at the most crucial point of impression, into the world-narrative. Scholars speak of the gospel as recording the end-in-the-process-of-realizing-itself. But the end is not yet, and it says that also. It stands at the moment of transition between the main body of history and the end of history; and what it says has a powerful effect on both. In this respect, as I've said, the "little apocalypse" of Chapter 13 is a model of the whole; before it stands a narrative of obscure organization; after it comes the well-formed and completive Passion story. So the gospel stands between past and immediately future time, establishing a continuity which makes sense only in terms of that which interrupts it. All Mark's minor intercalations reflect the image of a greater intervention represented by the whole book. And all such lesser interventions deepen and complicate the sense of the narrative; or, they are indications that more story is needed, as a supplement, if the story is to make sense.

Once we begin to look at matters in this way we shall find no lack of density and occult relation. The episode that precedes the double narrative of the little girl and the sick woman, as they take their complementary ways out of sickness into society, out of the unclean into the clean, is the story of the Gerasene demoniac. This too is an unusually elaborate narrative, and once more it seems to have embarrassed Matthew. The demoniac, presumably Gentile, is possessed by an unclean spirit, named Legion, who, as is the custom of unclean spirits in Mark, at once recognizes Jesus as the son of God. (It could almost be said that in this text such recognition is possible only to the unclean.) Mark emphasizes the enormous strength of the madman; Matthew leaves that out. In Mark he haunts tombs, and no chain or fetter can bind him: "night and day among the tombs and on the mountains he was always crying out and bruising himself with stones." When Legion is expelled, he, or they, occupy a herd of swine, which promptly destroys itself. This cure promotes terror among the Gerasenes, who implore Jesus to go away. He does so, leaving the madman cured and docile, "clothed and in his right mind"; but he tells the man, whom he will not allow to accompany him, to proclaim his cure (the parents of the dead girl were forbidden to do so, as is more usual in Mark).

The Gerasene displayed a demonic excess of male strength, but his violence leaves him with the unclean spirit — that it goes into pigs merely confirms its uncleanliness. The man is now ordered and civil; formerly naked he is now dressed, formerly dangerous in his strength he is now fit for society. In the case of the woman with the hemorrhage the going-out of power into the unclean was effected through a garment; here the going-out of strength with spirit (this time unclean) is signaled by the adoption of clothes. The tombs are unclean; the man, now healthy, leaves them. He is free of the unclean spirit (to pneuma akatharton) and from the unclean place (en katharo, "away from the defilement of dead bodies") and wears an unsoiled garment (katharos). This is a Gentile cure, as the other was Jewish (Jairus was a "ruler of the synagogue"). In both there is an emission of spirits, clean and unclean. One is followed by an injunction to proclaim, the other by a command to silence. One cure is of an excess of maleness, the other of related effects of femaleness. The lake divides the two like a slash, and the cured demoniac is forbidden to cross it.

These are suggestions — and some may think they are occasionally on the wild side — as to modes of interpretation, mere preliminaries to divination, no more. But they are needed, for the commentators often ask the kind of question found, on these occasions, in the mouths of the disciples. Taylor credits the story of the demoniac with a certain literary felicity, but at once ascribes this to accident, which enables him to drop the subject.[13] Another commentator remarks that "a measure of sober rationalizing might be in place here";[14] others provide it, or break the passage into pieces, or rewrite it: for example, the injunction to proclaim the cure is converted into a command to be silent — not because there is anything in the text to support such a change, but because the command to silence is more usual in Mark, and the usual is easier to handle.

An example of what may be done by a methodical refusal to countenance such practices may be found in Jean Starobinski's analysis of the story of the Gerasene demoniac. He takes the text as it is, deliberately ignoring any deformation attributable to its historical transmission, and — without pretending never to have read or heard any of the scholarship that has accumulated round the topic — tries to interpret what is written rather than what it is written about. He suggests that an outsider may see what escapes the exegete *de métier,* for example by declining to situate the narrative in historic time, that is, by treating it simply as narrative, rather than as a report — a report, moreover, of events more significant than any narrative of them. Such a study will not attempt to decompose the text, but will treat it in its entirety.

Starobinski believes that a text will offer, at some point, a hint — an index or emblem of the whole — as a guide to our reading of the whole; a modern variant of the Diltheyan *Eindruckspunkt* of which I spoke earlier. He finds this emblem in the concluding injunction to proclaim the cure. The demoniac is able to do so because he no longer yells and shrieks, but rationally announces. From his freedom — a freedom to be naked among the tombs, and to scream, *une liberté pour rien* — he passes to the constraints of clothes, houses, and proclamation. There is, at every level from the lexical to the thematic, a pattern of oppositions: between Jesus and the crowd, from which he withdraws but which he rejoins; between upper and lower worlds, god and demon. Even a single word, Legion (which the devils possessing the demoniac give as their name), is singular but collective ("My name is Legion, for we are many"); and the very prepositions replicate the antitheses of the grosser structure.[15]

Narrative analyses of this kind are less unusual than they were, for younger biblical scholars have adopted (sometimes, I think, too clinically) structuralist methods; but it is astonishing how much less there is of genuine literary criticism on the secular model than there ought to be. The practice has its dangers; Starobinski observes that "the danger of immanentist analysis certainly resides in its too great receptivity." This is true, though the decision as to what is too great and what too little is one that has, in the end, to be taken by institutional

consensus; and at present we are waiting for this consensus
to re-form after the quasi-revolutionary incursions of the recent
past.

It seems useless, therefore, to predict the fate of Starobinski's
method or mine, which is different, but which depends equally
on the effectiveness of its difference from the methods of the
insiders. I have been proposing that the device of intercalation
in Mark's narrative is an emblem of many conjunctions and
oppositions, which are found at all levels of the discourse. Like
Starobinski, I think these should be attended to, and not dis-
solved by recognitive hermeneutical tricks; for these conjunctions and oppositions reflect something of what the gospel
presupposes of its own structure, and the structure of the
world. The pursuit of such interpretations is not merely a matter of method; there has also to be divination, and divination
is an art related only very dubiously to rules. When Eliot said
that the only method was to be very intelligent he was both
exaggerating and saying too little. Method, he meant, is secondary, for first there must be divination. Having divined, you
must say something by way of explaining or communicating
the experience of that bewildering minute, and then method
is useful. Of course, no divination is adequate to the whole task
of interpretation; it may only record a radiance. And how
could one hope to hold in a single thought the whole of a text
so full of obscure relations, so rich in secrecy, as Mark? Interpreters must not be as confident as Macbeth that "augures" and
understood relations will bring forth the secret — only that
there *are* augures, and relations that may be understood.

BEING NOW so near an end, I am obliged to say something of
the whole of Mark, and the obscure relations that are there,
however deceptively, to be understood. Some kinds of speculation I shall forbid myself. I shall not peer into the past for a
glimpse of a man writing, out of a need I cannot know, a book
of which the content derived from perhaps a few pieces of
paper, and a quantity of oral material organized on principles
that must be guessed at, and ordering his material on some
principle (catchwords, topics, the requirements of a lectionary)

which seems not to have been in any easy sense biographical, yet involved something recognizable, in parts at any rate, as a narrative. It is not even a matter of guessing why, unlike all the others, he began with the Baptism, and ended, as they did not, with an empty tomb. We cannot discover whether his contemporaries thought his first thirteen chapters coherent in themselves, or an appropriate prologue to the Passion narrative. We gather that they found the book useful, at any rate for a while; but whatever we may find to say about the community for which it was originally written (and the evidence will come largely from the gospel itself, in defeating circularity) it is far beyond us to reproduce the tacit understandings that existed between this dead writer and his dead audience. Those accords are lost. We cannot know the original generic set of Mark; and to read it against our own is to read it differently. We have internalized expectations created by kinds of narrative, historical and fictive, and by kinds of poetry, quite unfamiliar to those original readers. We should remember this, and allow our sense of difference to exercise some control over our divinations; but in the end we have to think of the book as a sample of what we take literature to be, and avoid all the means by which that confrontation may be prevented.

Dozens of commentators have felt obliged to address the question of the literary structure of Mark. The results are not, it must be said, impressive. One critic does say that "Mark no more lends itself to analysis by means of a detailed outline developed by simple addition of components than does a major contrapuntal work of music"; but he retreats at once from this implied promise of serious analysis into speculative history.[16] Others have provided such an outline, and called it a structure. Many seem to hope that if the chronology and geography of the gospel can be made to seem plausible as part of a factual record, the narrative problems will go away. Or, causes quite external to the text are adduced for its being so deficient in the qualities ordinarily attributed to well-formed narrative.[17]

It is not surprising that all these accounts are different in detail; but there is one point of practically unanimous agreement, which is that the Marcan narrative has a major climax right in

the middle, at 8:27. It is the recognition by Peter of Jesus' messiahship. It produces the first of the three Passion predictions,
and begins a new movement, spiritually and geographically,
toward Jerusalem. It also follows hard upon the tale of Jesus
questioning the disciples in the boat, the riddle of the single
loaf which I discussed earlier (he accuses them of seeing without perceiving), and upon the remarkable story, omitted by
both Matthew and Luke, of the healing of a blind man by a
double application of spittle — after the first he can see men,
but only dimly, "like trees walking"; the second application
completes the cure.

Jesus accuses his followers of seeing without perceiving, like
the crowd of outsiders who are bewildered (and worse) by the
parables, and like the blind man after the first treatment. So
we think we know what to expect when he asks them another
question: "Who do men say that I am?" And sure enough, we
get a half-blind answer, which echoes the speculations at the
court of Herod earlier: John the Baptist, or Elijah, or a prophet.
But then Peter, as if suddenly enabled to perceive, says, "You
are the Christ."

Here, then, right in the middle of the book, is the great moment of recognition. But nobody subsequently behaves as if he
had benefited by it; and indeed its pleasures and promises are
instantly disappointed. Himself avoiding the word "Christ"
(Matthew would have none of this, and put the word in) Jesus
tells them sharply to keep silence on the matter. The verb even
suggests a rebuke. He then — "plainly," *parrēsia* — prophesies
his Passion. Whereupon Peter rebukes him (same verb). Mark
does not tell us for what (Matthew does: "God forbid, Lord!
This shall never happen to you"). Whatever Peter said earns
an even sterner rebuke (same verb): "Get behind me, Satan."
These words are used directly to the devil in Matthew's story
of the wilderness temptation, but Mark uses them only here.
Now for Matthew it may be said that this *is* a simple, crucial
point, for it is the moment of the declaration that the Church
will be built on Peter, the rock. Mark is much less simple. Later
his Jesus will declare himself the Christ, for the one and only
time, at the moment when Peter denies him. Here it is Peter

who makes the affirmation and is rebuked (as it were, denied) by Jesus, who withholds the word that Peter speaks. Thus is translated into narrative the schematic opposition of silence and proclamation. We find it in the parables, in the beginning of the gospel and in its end, as well as in intermediate narratives. And there are other, presumably related oppositions: election and rebuke, clean and unclean (for what Peter seems unable to accept is the prophecy of an unclean, criminal's death for Jesus), the things of God and the things of men (the latter associated with a wrong view of uncleanness).

If we decide that this passage really is the core of the text, we shall have to allow that there is mystery in it; we cannot use it simply as an explanation, as a piece of self-evident sense by which we can hope to decipher more enigmatic or ambiguous moments. Wrede's famous book on the Messianic secret[18] has now, after eighty years, lost its power to shock, and has been assimilated into the tradition it then confounded; it is fairly commonplace now to read in the commentators some expression of the view that the injunctions to secrecy are essential to the design of the work, which depends on the proposition that nothing can become clear until after the Resurrection. But the value of Wrede's theory is less that it explains how Mark's book came to be as it is (why he had to put in so much, and so oddly, about secrecy) than that it compels us to see what is actually there: the antithesis of silence and proclamation, and its relation to a whole network of disjunct but collocated qualities throughout the work.

Let me look briefly at Mark's resonant overture. Here is clear proclamation. Mark proclaims, "The beginning of the gospel of Jesus Christ, the son of God" (to take the fullest text); John the Baptist proclaims, "John the baptizer appeared in the wilderness, preaching a baptism of repentance." There follows a vivid portrait of John, carefully constructed in accordance with the type of Elijah, precursor of the Messiah, though Jesus, whose epiphany is secret and unproclaimed, is not described. After the Baptism the spirit drives Jesus into the wilderness, and when he returns he begins to preach, to proclaim, as if he were taking over John's task, though without use of baptism.

His authority (a quality on which Mark likes to insist) is widely recognized; his miraculous cures are seen by great crowds. But once again he withdraws (a repeated movement, which Starobinski calls *esseulement*).

Here already strong thematic oppositions are forming. John is associated with public baptism, the public fulfillment of his type, Elijah; Jesus with private epiphany and the private fulfillment of his type, Messiah. Moreover, Jesus accepts a baptism of repentance (suggesting prior uncleanness) and at the same time is called the son of God. The paradoxes continue: unmistakable public recognitions alternate with demands for and withdrawals into silence. Demons infallibly recognize him, disciples do not. The Law is now kept and now broken. The canons of purity are challenged; a purity which is itself accused of uncleanliness opposes and purges the unclean. If the general sense that there is a moment of special force in the eighth chapter is well founded, it must be so because so many of these paradoxes come together there in a great knot. But there are many knots; they occur in the riddling parables, in the frequent collocation of perceptive demons and imperceptive saints, in the delight and gratitude of the outsider who is cured, and the astonishment, fear, and dismay of the insiders.

We know by now that we must not look in Mark for those regular accumulations of narrative sense which we habitually regard as the marks of a well-formed narrative. Instead we are jostled from one puzzle to the next — immediately, again, *euthus, palin* — as if the purpose of the story were less to establish a comfortable sequence than to pile one crux on another, each instituting an intense thematic opposition. They differ in detail; they do not fit. But one is, as it were, deposited on top of the other, as if to form a sort of aniconic figure for meditative interpretation. A complex figure of this kind stands, as we have seen, at the very center of that part of the gospel which precedes the Passion narrative, where history-likeness and the powerful suggestion of complete and followable sequentiality take over. Up to that point we must read in a different way. The instant assembling and dismissal of crowds, the motiveless journeyings in and out, back and forth, up and down, do not have that kind of narrative value; they are rather the material of these inexplicit figurations, and behind them all we sense an algebra, some formal principle of opposition and contradiction.

Here is another instance of what happens when one such figure is superimposed on another. On two occasions Jesus visits his own town (Mark 3:19–35, 6:1–6). The first time he is accused by the scribes, but also by his own family,[19] of being mad, possessed by a demon (and therefore unclean). Part of the evidence for this is that he casts out demons. He refutes the charges in riddles, and utters a dark saying concerning the unforgivable sin, which is to blaspheme against the Holy Spirit by saying "he has an unclean spirit." Here, in sharp collision, are the Holy Spirit and the unclean spirit (the same word is used for both); it is the same opposition as we saw between clean and unclean in the story of the demoniac and the story of the woman with the hemorrhage. And because they confuse spirit with spirit, clean *pneuma* with unclean *pneuma*, his family is cast outside. In the second passage Jesus preaches to his townsmen and is heard at first with astonishment, but then with resentment, it seems because of his difference with his family. And he loses force — not usefully, as when the woman touched his garment, but in such a way that "he could do no mighty work"; "mighty work" is, once again, *dunamis*. Matthew did not like this way of putting it ("he did not do *many* mighty works," Matthew 13:58). Mark, as usual, is much bolder. The stock explanation is that the early church was always wondering how the Jews ever came to reject Jesus. But that really is dodging. The family, by confusing clean and unclean, became outsiders; but the blasphemous confusion is damaging, and results in a loss of force. By resolving this double image into a narrative I have brought it close to the point where it would become susceptible of psychoanalytic interpretation. All I wish to say, though, is that there is, in the superimposition, something to interpret.

It would be possible, I think, to make a case for the Transfiguration as the central knot in the narrative, not only because of its ironies — the conjunction of revealed mystery, Moses and Elijah and Jesus in gleaming unearthly white, and the silliness of Peter, who wants to bustle about building them shelters; but also because of the sudden disappearance of Jesus and the others, leaving alone on a bare mountain the three great insiders, Peter and James and John, who had seen but not perceived, heard but not understood, the sight and sounds of heaven. Later they are enjoined, quite unnecessarily, to silence. Mystery and stupidity make an important conjunction or opposition; but it must be seen with all the others, denial and recognition, silence and proclamation, clean and unclean, indoors and out, lake and mountain, one side and the other side. Even the apocalypse is both now, and to come. And we know that at the end of the book the resurrection is proclaimed to those who keep silence, from a place that is within doors yet open, since the stone has been rolled back; it is a tomb but it contains an unrecognized young man who reminds us of the one who ran away; he is not naked, like the demoniac in his tombs, but civilly clothed, like the demoniac cured; in a place normally unclean but now clean he proclaims, he does not shriek. This mystery is confronted with stupid silence.

We know certain things about Mark: we know, for instance, that we cannot treat this gospel as a work of irony or a confidence trick. We disallow the possibility that it has the character of Defoe's *The Shortest Way with the Dissenters* or Samuel Butler's *Fair Haven*, both of which could be and were read in senses opposite to those intended. But we do so only because of what we have been taught. We have acquired fore-understandings which exclude such readings. This is a benefit, no doubt; but the generic forces that confer it may also prematurely limit the possible senses of the work.[20] We are most unwilling to accept mystery, what cannot be reduced to other and more intelligible forms. Yet that is what we find here: something irreducible, therefore perpetually to be interpreted; not secrets to be found out one by one, but Secrecy.

Perhaps that secrecy is nothing more than our own bewilderment projected into the text. Do we project into it our deafness and blindness? People have found secrecy there, though in different forms, from the beginning. There were secrets expounded only to the initiate, for it was believed that the writers of scripture had themselves practiced what Clement called a "prophetic and venerable system of concealment." [21] And, as we have seen, there were secret versions of the text. Even the contradictions and discrepancies between the gospels became mysteries; Origen thought they were put there deliberately to exercise the pious interpreter. At Qumran, as well as in Christian communities, this attribution of mystery to the sacred texts was unquestioned. Once a text is credited with high authority it is studied intensely; once it is so studied it acquires mystery or secrecy. The tradition undergoes many transformations, but is continuous; revivals of learning did not destroy but fostered secrecy, and the Renaissance cult of esoteric wisdom survived the new literalism of Reform. The belief that a text might be an open proclamation, available to all, coexisted comfortably with the belief that it was a repository of secrets. And this quality of sacred books is inherited by their counterparts in the secular canon. Shakespeare is an inexhaustible source of occult readings — even, to cite the most vulgar instance, of ciphered senses; yet at the same time he is believed to speak plainly, about most of human life, to any literate layman. Like the scriptures, he is open to all, but at the same time so dark that special training, organized by an institution of considerable size, is required for his interpretation. Nor is the belief that the true sense is hidden confined to professional corporations, with vested interests; Freud knew, when he wrote *The Interpretation of Dreams*, that the hypothesis of latent sense was one he shared, not with his colleagues and the authors of the scientific literature on dreams to which he alludes so patiently, but with most of the remainder of mankind through the centuries.

What is the interpreter to make of secrecy considered as a property of all narrative, provided it is suitably attended to? Outsiders see but do not perceive. Insiders read and perceive, but always in a different sense. We glimpse the secrecy through the meshes of a text; this is divination, but what is divined is what is visible from our angle. It is a momentary radiance, delusive or not, as in Kafka's parable. When we come to relate that part to the whole, the divined glimmer to the fire we suppose to be its source, we see why Hermes is the patron of so many other trades besides interpretation. There has to be trickery. And we interpret always as transients — of whom he is also patron — both in the book and in the world which resembles the book. For the world is our beloved codex. We may not see it, as Dante did, in perfect order, gathered by love into one volume; but we do, living as reading, like to think of it as a place where we can travel back and forth at will, divining congruences, conjunctions, opposites; extracting secrets from its secrecy, making understood relations, an appropriate algebra. This is the way we satisfy ourselves with explanations of the unfollowable world — as if it were a structured narrative, of which more might always be said by trained readers of it, by insiders. World and book, it may be, are hopelessly plural, endlessly disappointing; we stand alone before them, aware of their arbitrariness and impenetrability, knowing that they may be narratives only because of our impudent intervention, and susceptible of interpretation only by our hermetic tricks. Hot for secrets, our only conversation may be with guardians who know less and see less than we can; and our sole hope and pleasure is in the perception of a momentary radiance, before the door of disappointment is finally shut on us.

Notes

I. Carnal and Spiritual Senses

1. London, 1939.
2. See N. O. Brown, *Hermes the Thief*, Madison, 1947. On "boundary-crosser (*trēktēr*), see p. 44.
3. *Paris Review*, 19 (1958): 60f.
4. Wilhelm Dilthey, *Gesammelte Schriften*, Stuttgart, 1913–58, vols. V, VI (*Die geistige Welt*). Dilthey believes that the artist unifies disparate impressions of reality around such a point; the counterpart of the *gefühlter Eindruckspunkt* in ordinary life is a dominant trait, for example the human face. Other impressions converge round this central one. For Dilthey this point, which gives articulation to the whole, is, whether in life or art, the product of him who understands; that is, the artist's activity is the origin of the impression-point. He was obviously not considering the possibility that a work of art is the kind of "world" in which other impression-points than the one he associates with the mental constitution of the artist might be taken as the starting-point of interpretative articulations; and *a fortiori* it did not occur to him that the impression-point speciously indicated by the text was the very one that interpretation ought to ignore, as many modern practitioners would hold. There is a clear exposition of Dilthey's doctrine in Kurt Müller-Vollmer, *Towards a Phenomenological Theory of Literature: A Study of Wilhelm Dilthey's Poetik*, The Hague, 1963, especially Chapter 8. According to later hermeneutic theorists, Dilthey's assumption that the interpreter must strive to concern himself only with historical understanding, setting aside his own "prejudices," is false; in its extreme form the later doctrine maintains that it is precisely in his historical difference that the interpreter finds his power.

5. See J. Habermas, *Knowledge and Human Interests*, translated by Jeremy Shapiro, Boston, 1971, Chapters 10–12.

6. This was the position of Antioch against Alexandria, and it is forcefully expressed by Theodore of Mopsuestia in his *Commentary on Galatians 4:24*. Claiming that his opponents (in Alexandria) distort the sense of Paul's "these things are said allegorically," he asserts that "their wish is to deny any difference between the whole of the history recorded in divine Scripture and dreams that occur at night. Adam, they say, is not Adam — this being a place where they are especially prone to interpret divine Scripture in a spiritual way (spiritual interpretation is what they like to have their nonsense called) — paradise is not paradise and the serpent not a serpent. What I would like to say in reply to them is that once they start removing bits of history they will be left without any history at all. In that case they must tell us how they will be in a position to say who was the first man to be created or how man came to be disobedient or how the sentence of death was introduced. If it is from the Scriptures that they have learnt their answers to these questions, it follows that their talk of 'allegory' is obvious nonsense, because it is clearly irrelevant at all these points. If on the other hand they are right, and what is written is not a record of things that happened but is a pointer to some other profound truth in need of interpretation — some spiritual truth it may be, to use a phrase they like, which they have grasped through being such spiritual people themselves — then they must tell us by what means they have acquired these notions." (Translated by Maurice Wiles and Mark Santer in their *Documents in Early Christian Thought*, Cambridge, 1975, pp. 151–152.) It should perhaps be added that the proneness of allegorists to excess was also noted and reproved in Judaism. The extremists were tolerated, but "allegorical" came to be considered the antonym of "literal" meaning (see J. Z. Lauterbach, "Ancient Jewish Allegorists," *Jewish Quarterly Review*, new series 1 (1910): 291–333, 503–553.

For the original transformation of Torah into Old Testament see Hans von Campenhausen, *The Formation of the Christian Bible*, translated by J. A. Baker, Philadelphia, 1972.

7. See J. S. Preus, *From Shadow to Promise: Old Testament Interpretation from Augustine to the Young Luther*, Cambridge, Mass., 1969, p. 72f.

8. An authoritative brief account of the origins and influence of the Joachimite doctrines is Marjorie Reeves, *Joachim of Fiore and the Prophetic Future*, London, 1976.

II. Hoti's Business: Why Are Narratives Obscure?

1. The answer is: two in the front, three in the back.
2. Franz Kafka, *Parables and Paradoxes* (bilingual ed.), New York, 1961, pp. 92–93.
3. *Parables and Paradoxes*, pp. 60–79.
4. "The seed is the Word: yet the crop which comes up is composed of various classes of people." (C. H. Dodd, *The Parables of the Kingdom*, rev. ed., New York, 1961, p. 3.) Dodd of course believes that the allegorical reading came in later and belongs to a different *Sitz im Leben*. "The probability is that the parables could have been taken for allegorical mystifications only in a non-Jewish environment. Among Jewish teachers the parable was a common and well-understood method of illustration, and the parables of Jesus are similar in form to Rabbinic parables. The question therefore, why He taught in parables, would not be likely to arise, still less to receive such a perplexing answer. In the Hellenistic world, on the other hand, the use of myths, allegorically interpreted, as vehicles of esoteric doctrine was widespread, and something of the kind would be looked for from Christian teachers. It was this, as much as anything, which set interpretation going on wrong lines" (pp. 4–5). The attitude of J. Jeremias, *The Parables of Jesus*, rev. ed., London, 1963, is not very different. These opinions continue to prevail in various modified forms, but they have been cogently questioned; and recently John Drury has shown pretty conclusively that they cannot be right — *Journal of Theological Studies*, new series 24 (1973): 367–379. The Jewish parable could certainly be allegorical and deliberately obscure (cf. Ezekiel), and there is no historical reason to believe that the parables of Jesus could not have been riddling or enigmatic from the beginning. Moreover it was common rabbinical practice to offer private interpretations to favored insiders, and Dodd was wrong to suppose that the privileged explanations of the Sower Parable and of the saying about "things that come out of a man" (Mark, 7) are necessarily later accretions (D. Daube, "Public Retort and Private Explanation," in *The New Testament and Rabbinical Judaism*, London, 1956, pp. 141–150). Finally, it is possible to argue that although the outsiders could not have access to the mystery, the parables were intended to provide them with the best possible substitute; far from being intended to baffle, the parables had senses that yielded themselves to reflection. Only if one saw and heard, but failed to go beyond that, could it be said that one had avoided turning to be forgiven. See J. Bowker, *Journal of Theological Studies*, new series 25 (1974): 300–317.

5. V. Taylor, *The Gospel According to St. Mark: The Greek Text with Introduction, Notes and Indexes*, 2nd ed., New York, 1966, p. 257. C. E. B. Cranfield, *The Gospel According to St. Mark* (*The Cambridge Greek Testament Commentary*), ed. of 1972, pp. 155f, also accepts *hina* as "in order that," pointing out that the philological evidence for other senses is trifling in comparison to the contextual evidence in favor of the harder interpretation; "in order that" he says, "reflects the teleological thinking which is characteristic of the whole of the Bible, including the Synoptic Gospels" Jeremias, pp. 13f, accepts *hina* in the same sense, but thinks the free quotation from Isaiah should be given in quotation marks, with this effect: "in order that (as it is written) they 'may see and not see, etc.' " Jeremias thinks *mēpote* means "unless" (p. 17). Dodd (p. 3n) argues that the crucial passage contains so many words not found elsewhere in the synoptics, but usual in Paul, that it must be apostolic rather than primitive. Jeremias (pp. 77f) makes a similar point.

6. Albert Schweitzer, *The Quest of the Historical Jesus*, translated by W. Montgomery, New York, ed. of 1968, p. 263.

7. It is neither desirable nor possible to report all the arguments about this passage, which are very learned and complex. But I should add that Mark's version of Isaiah 6:9f corresponds to neither the Hebrew nor the Septuagint text; yet it agrees with the Targum (Aramaic version) and this may be thought, since the Targum was used in the synagogue, to support the argument for its historical authenticity (Jeremias, p. 15). Jeremias, however, believes (and he is not alone) that although authentic the logion has got into the wrong place, and probably belongs to the second half of the gospel; Mark, perhaps misled by a catchword (*parabolē*) put it in this sequence of parables, though originally it was an expression, of a not unfamiliar kind, of a general disillusionment, and had nothing to do with the interpretation of parables or the reason for teaching in parables. Matthew's version of the Isaiah quotation exactly reproduces the Septuagint, and gives the whole thing in its original second-person form; it is as if Matthew, as he worried over Mark's text, checked the quotation in his Greek Bible and found that version more congenial. But I am told that the Hebrew of Isaiah supports the purposive sense of *hina*.

8. See Dan O. Via, *The Parables: Their Literary and Existential Dimensions*, Philadelphia, 1967.

9. See J. D. Kingsbury, *Matthew: Structure, Christology, Kingdom*, Philadelphia, 1975.

10. See Taylor, *Mark*, p. 256, and Jeremias (note 7 above).

11. See R. P. C. Hanson, *Allegory and Event*, London, 1959, p. 76n. J. Daniélou, *History of Early Christian Doctrine*, translated by J. A. Baker, London, 1973, II, 13, believes this to have been the dominical interpretation.

12. *The Cambridge History of the Bible*, I, ed. P. R. Ackroyd and C. F. Evans, Cambridge, 1970, 417. (Henceforth *CHB*.)

13. *Parables of the Kingdom*, pp. 1–2, which treats this interpretation as characteristic of the allegorical epoch.

14. For Augustine on the Good Samaritan see Sermon lxxxi, in *Select Library of Nicene and Post-Nicene Fathers*, ed. P. Schaff, ed. of 1974, vol. VI, and *Quaestiones Evangeliorum*, II, 19; for the interpretation of the Feeding, see *Homilies on John*, Oxford, 1848, Homily xxiv, I, 375f.

15. G. R. Owst, *Literature and Pulpit in Medieval England*, Cambridge, 1933; ed. of 1961, pp. 58–59.

16. Owst, p. 62.

17. See the detailed discussion in Jeremias, *Parables*, pp. 202f; where, incidentally, the circumstances in which the parable came to be told are interpreted differently.

18. B. Gerhardsson, *The Good Samaritan — the Good Shepherd?*, Lund, 1958. An entirely different set of Old Testament models is proposed by J. Drury, *Tradition and Design in Luke's Gospel*, London, 1976, pp. 77f.

19. H. Conzelmann, *The Theology of St. Luke*, New York, 1960, p. 72.

20. H.-G. Gadamer, *Truth and Method*, London, 1975, p. 264.

21. "The Origin of the Work of Art," in *Poetry, Language and Thought*, translated and edited by Albert Hofstadter, New York, 1960, pp. 15–87.

22. New York, 1966.

23. Paul Ricoeur, "What is a Text?", in David M. Rasmussen, ed., *Mythic-Symbolic Language and Philosophical Anthropology*, The Hague, 1971.

24. Jeremias, *Parables*, pp. 70f; Dodd, *Parables* (with variations of detail), pp. 96f.

25. Paul Ricoeur, "Biblical Hermeneutics," *Semeia*, 4 (1975): 29–148. The second issue of *Semeia* (1974) is devoted to analysis of parables, especially The Good Samaritan.

26. See D. P. Walker, "Esoteric Symbolism," in *Poetry and Poetics from Ancient Greece to the Renaissance*, Ithaca, 1975, pp. 218–231.

27. For an elaborate interpretation of this passage in the context

of the gospel as a whole, see Q. Quesnell, *The Mind of Mark: Interpretation and Method through the Exegesis of Mark: 6.52*, Analecta Biblica 38, Rome, 1969.

III. The Man in the Macintosh, the Boy in the Shirt

1. Stuart Gilbert, *James Joyce's Ulysses*, New York, 1931, pp. 152f. Gilbert got the idea from Victor Bérard's *Les Phéniciens et l'Odyssée*, in which all the mysterious movements of Theoclymenos are set forth, with the speculation that he may have been a hero in a part of the epic cycle following the *Odyssey* — the *Telegony*.
2. Stanislaus Joyce, *My Brother's Keeper*, New York, 1958, p. 165; and articles by John O. Lyons (in *James Joyce Miscellany*, 2nd series, London, 1959, pp. 133f) and by Thomas E. Connolly (in *James Joyce's Dubliners*, ed. Clive Hart, London, 1969, pp. 107f).
3. Robert M. Adams, *Surface and Symbol*, New York, 1962, pp. 218, 245–246. Hélène Cixous, *The Exile of James Joyce*, translated by Sally A. J. Purcell, New York, 1972, expressly disagrees with Adams, saying that by the time the table emits its loud lone crack Bloom "knows . . . who M'Intosh was . . . The garment has become transparent to Bloom's 'unconscious substance,' and he has now to struggle against the truth that is self-imposed" (712f). How *we* know this is not explained.
4. Note the persistent suppression of Bloom's name in the concluding pages of "Cyclops." Indeed, as Gilbert points out, "the idea of anonymity or misnomer is suggested under many aspects" — perhaps by way of allusion to Odysseus' change of name to No-man in the relevant episode of Homer (*James Joyce's Ulysses*, p. 252).
5. Adams, *Surface and Symbol*, p. 186.
6. *The Pleasure of the Text*, translated by Richard Miller, New York, 1975, p. 11.
7. Thomas Kuhn, *The Structure of Scientific Revolutions*, 2nd ed., Chicago, 1970.
8. Taylor, *St. Mark*, pp. 561–562.
9. Cranfield, *St. Mark*, p. 438.
10. Taylor, *St. Mark*, p. 561, Cranfield, *St. Mark*, p. 438.
11. Quoted by H. Jonas, *The Gnostic Religion*, 2nd ed. rev., Boston, 1963, p. 274. Jonas, describing the Gnostic "Hymn of the Pearl" or "Song of the Apostle Judas Thomas," mentions that the symbolism of a garment includes a use of it as the heavenly or ideal double of

a person on earth, sometimes the Saviour. That an allegory of Gnostic origin has been intruded at this point in the Passion narrative has not, so far as I know, been proposed by the exegetes, who may well find it wholly counter-intuitive.

12. Morton Smith, *Clement of Alexandria and a Secret Gospel of Mark*, Cambridge, Mass., 1973; *The Secret Gospel*, London, 1974.

13. Austin Farrer, *A Study in St. Mark*, London, 1951; *St. Matthew and St. Mark*, 1954 (2nd ed., 1966).

14. For the view that Peter's third denial is a formal curse directed against Jesus, see Helmut Merkel, "Peter's Curse," *The Trial of Jesus*, ed. Ernst Bammel (Studies in Biblical Theology, second series, 13), London, 1970, pp. 66–71.

15. Schweitzer, *The Quest of the Historical Jesus*, p. 4.

16. For the difficulties that arise when "history-likeness" is confused with historical reference, see Hans Frei, *The Eclipse of Biblical Narrative*, New Haven, 1974.

17. Richard Ellmann, *James Joyce*, New York, 1959, p. 535. He also told Samuel Beckett "I may have oversystematized *Ulysses*" (Ellmann, p. 715).

18. "La Construction de la nouvelle et du roman," in T. Todorov ed. *Théorie de la littérature: Textes des Formalistes russes*, Paris, 1965, pp. 170–196.

19. D. E. Nineham, *Saint Mark* (Pelican Gospel Commentaries), Harmondsworth, 1963, p. 439.

20. Ellmann, *James Joyce*, p. 536.

21. Ellmann, p. 725. (Translation slightly altered.)

22. J. Jeremias, *The Eucharistic Words of Jesus*, translated by Norman Perrin, London, 1966, p. 132.

23. W. L. Knox, quoted in Taylor, *St. Mark*, p. 609.

24. Farrer, *Study*, p. 174.

25. Jonathan Culler, *Structuralist Poetics*, London, 1975, p. 244.

26. Etienne Trocmé, *The Formation of the Gospel According to Mark*, translated by Pamela Gaughan, London, 1975, p. 240.

IV. Necessities of Upspringing

1. Preface to *The Portrait of a Lady* (1906), in *The Art of the Novel*, ed. R. P. Blackmur, New York, 1934, pp. 42–48.

2. Although Aristotle is somewhat terse and obscure on the issue, it is clear that he gave priority to action over character; the latter is

included for the sake of the former. "He wants to make the proposition that character serves action seem no less assured than is (for a Greek) the proposition that the only legitimate use of colour in painting is to support the finished likeness," as John Jones puts it in his admirably argued discussion of the point (On Aristotle and Greek Tragedy, London, 1962, p. 31). For Aristotle character (ēthos) is "that which reveals a moral choice," and a sequence of moral choices is an action.

3. "Esquisse de conclusion," in Exégèse et herméneutique, ed. X. Léon-Dufour, Paris, 1971, p. 285.

4. V. Propp, Morphology of Folktale, translated by L. Scott, Bloomington, 1958.

5. A. J. Greimas, Sémantique structurale, Paris, 1966.

6. Daniel Patte, What Is Structuralist Interpretation? Philadelphia, 1976, p. 43.

7. For a hostile critique, see Jonathan Culler, Structuralist Poetics, pp. 75f.

8. Though some believe Luke's narrative to be independent of Mark's. See W. G. Kümmel, Introduction to the New Testament, translated by Howard C. Kee from the 17th German edition of 1973, London, 1975, pp. 131–132, for lists of those who accept and reject independence. J. Jeremias, The Eucharistic Words of Jesus, translated by Norman Perrin from the 3rd German edition of 1964, Philadelphia, 1977, also thinks Luke independent (p. 99).

9. Kahler was writing in 1860. See Howard C. Kee, Community of the New Age, London, 1977, p. 30, and nn. 78–80 (p. 186).

10. See G. Vermes, "Bible and Midrash," in CHB, I (1970), 199f, and Scripture and Tradition in Judaism, Leiden, 1961; John Drury, Tradition and Design in Luke's Gospel, London, 1976, pp. 5f; and the bibliography in Raymond E. Brown, The Birth of the Messiah, New York, 1977, p. 563. The fullest bibliography is in an important but as yet unpublished article by David Stern, "Midrash: a Bibliographical Survey." In his comments Stern considers the objection made by some scholars that midrash, as we know it, could not have existed before A.D. 70, since the rabbinical technique was developed some time after that date. On this strict view there is no midrash in the Old Testament or in the New. But the problem is really one of terminology, since, as Stern remarks, it cannot be doubted that midrash-like writing occurs in both, whether we want to call it midrash, proto-midrash, or something else. Stern, in fact, finds the New Testament to be more in the manner of the sort of redaction he calls "re-written biblical narrative." The gospels contain midrashic elements but are less

innovative and revolutionary than the midrash; indeed he describes them as in this light "deeply conservative, even anachronistic."

11. C. H. Roberts, in *CHB*, I, 53.

12. The description of the Qumran manuscript as a collection of testimonies is thought doubtful by Brown, *Birth of the Messiah*, p. 101, n10.

13. See M. D. Goulder, *Midrash and Lection in Matthew*, London, 1974.

14. See Drury, *Tradition and Design*.

15. See Brown, *The Birth of the Messiah*.

16. C. H. Dodd, *Historical Tradition in the Fourth Gospel*, Cambridge, 1963, p. 29.

17. Jeremias, *Eucharistic Words of Jesus*, p. 96.

18. As Louis Marin puts it, he is the agent by whose act it becomes possible for God to die. "The death of God is necessary and impossible; someone must make it necessary, possible: how? By the random act of treachery ... The traitor is the necessity of a logic of narrative that has to solve an impossible problem." *Sémiotique de la Passion*, Paris, 1971, 106f (my translation).

19. He makes it a Passover meal and includes an account of the preparations for it. Many difficulties arise from a consideration of the historicity of the meal as Mark records it — when was it taken? How was it related to the Passover? — but these we may pass by. It may be, as Jeremias holds, that there is a reference to a Christianized version of the Passover; that this may explain the eucharistic words, ultimately based on the Passover formulas. Like the Jews, the early Christians thought of Passover as the probable time of the Messiah's coming, though they awaited the hour fasting rather than feasting, in order to distinguish their specific hope of Parousia from the less focused aspirations of the Jews (Jeremias, *Eucharistic Words*, pp. 123f). On the other hand, the imperfections of the account, considered as relating to some kind of Passover meal, may simply indicate a sketchiness in the fitting of the testimony of the shared bread into the narrative. See also T. A. Burkill, *Mysterious Revelation*, Ithaca, 1963.

20. Jeremias suggests that Jesus' words imply "I go to death as the true Passover sacrifice" (p. 224).

21. It was generally thought that the Psalmist, in the testimony (41:9), was referring to Achitophel, which would facilitate Matthew's transition to 2 Samuel.

22. F. J. F. Jackson and Kirsopp Lake, *The Beginnings of Christianity*, Part I, London, 1933, pp. 22–30; Pierre Benoit, "The Death

of Judas," in *Jesus and the Gospel*, I, translated by Benet Wetherhead from *Exégèse et Théologie*, I, London, 1973, pp. 189–207.

23. See C. H. Roberts in *CHB*, I, 48f; B. M. Metzger, *The Text of the New Testament*, 2nd ed., New York, 1977, pp. 6f; for a further opinion that the evangelists could have used the codex from the outset, see Saul Lieberman, "Jewish and Christian Codices," in *Hellenism in Jewish Palestine*, New York, 1950, pp. 203f.

24. I used these terms in *The Sense of an Ending*, New York, 1967, when I noted that James Barr, in *Biblical Words for Time*, London, 1962 (pp. 20f), issued a caveat against the too antithetical use of the words.

25. Mark 14:62. Some witnesses read *su eipas hoti egō eimi*, "You have said that I am," and this more characteristic reading is easier to understand as the basis of Matthew 26:64 and Luke 22:70. Taylor, in his edition of the Greek text (New York, 1952, 2nd ed. 1966) seems inclined to accept the longer reading, and so does Cranfield in his Cambridge Greek Testament commentary, 1959, ed. of 1973. From the narrative point of view the received reading (simply *egō eimi*, I am) is stronger, partly because it *is* unexpected, partly because of the counterpoint with Peter's denial.

26. Matt. 26:50: *hetaire, eph' ho parei?*

27. Jeremias, *Eucharistic Words of Jesus*, p. 54.

28. See Chapter Three above.

29. J. Betz, reported in Jeremias, p. 83.

30. Paul Winter, *On the Trial of Jesus*, 2nd ed., *Studia Judaica*, Band I, Berlin and New York, 1974, pp. 196, 198.

31. See P. F. Baum, "The English Ballad of Judas Iscariot," *Publications of the Modern Language Association*, 31 (1916): 181–189; P. Dronke, *The Medieval Lyric*, New York, 1969, p. 67–69; D. G. Schueler, "The Middle English *Judas*: An Interpretation," *PMLA* 91 (1976): 840–845.

32. C. K. Barrett, ed., *New Testament Background: Selected Documents*, London, 1956, ed. of 1974, p. 206.

33. Drury, *Tradition and Design*, p. 113.

34. Drury suggests that this rapprochement between Jewish and Gentile leaders is "theologically and morally effective" (p. 112) because it occurs "on the very day of the shedding of Christ's blood" (p. 17). His whole treatment of Luke's midrashic rewriting of the Marcan Passion narrative is full of interest.

35. For the Pilate fantasies, see A. Roberts and J. Donaldson, ed.

Apocryphal Gospels, Acts and Revelations, Ante-Nicene Christian Library, vol. XVI, Edinburgh, 1870. For the Magnificat as midrash, see Drury, p. 58.

36. A point made sharply by G. Vermes in "Bible and Midrash," *CHB,* I, 199f.

V. What Precisely Are the Facts?

1. Morton White, *Foundations of Historical Knowledge,* New York, 1965, p. 222. According to White, a "history" is distinguished from "chronicle" in the first place by its containing causal statements. The truth of history is determined by the truth of its components alone, but the *value* of history is affected by the metahistorical value judgment which governs the historian's choice of chronicle. Such judgments belong not to the chronicle but to the historian in his own time, and may be made consciously — with a view to providing explanations of the events of that time — or arrived at by some process resembling that which R. G. Collingwood (*The Idea of History,* Oxford, 1946) calls "re-enactment," that action of the writer's mind upon past thought without which history does not exist. White's account of the categories of metahistorically motivated choices is touched on below.

The models of historical explanation offered by Hayden White (*Metahistory,* Baltimore, 1973) are Formist, Organicist, Mechanistic, and Contextualist; but none of them, so far as I can see, will work with the texts here considered. One would need to add a fifth, called, perhaps, Hermeneutic (for reasons given in this chapter). Modern instances of it might be hard to find outside the historico-prophetic works of pyramidologists, Seventh Day Adventists or other fundamentalist and apocalyptic sects, of which, however, there are nowadays a great number.

2. Hans von Campenhausen argues that John, unlike the synoptics, treated these Old Testament oracles as a "conventional theological exercise" — he had a deeper sense of the Old Testament as profoundly christological; therefore he did not "accumulate further 'proofs' of this sort" (*The Formation of the Christian Bible,* translated by J. A. Baker, Philadelphia, 1972, pp. 55, 57). But the passage under discussion seems to be precisely such an accumulation, and it is peculiar to John. All agree that the allusion to the spear thrust in some texts of Matthew (27:49) is a late addition, and taken from John.

It hardly needs saying that scholarly comment on the passage is voluminous and refined. On possible interpretations of verse 35 (the intrusive affirmation of veracity) see R. Brown, *The Gospel According to John*, XIII–XXI (Anchor Bible, 29a, New York, 1966), pp. 936–937. On the testimonies of verses 36–37 see Brown, pp. 937–938. Brown also has an extensive discussion of the symbolism of the events described (948–956), and this has a bearing on the use and adaptation of the verses from Psalms, Zechariah, Exodus, and Numbers, as well as of other possible Old Testament sources.

3. Erich Auerbach, *Mimesis*, Princeton, 1953, Chapter II; and, on *sermo humilis*, *Literary Language and Its Public in Late Latin Antiquity and in the Middle Ages*, New York, 1965.

4. Brown, *St. John*, p. 935.

5. See A. T. Hanson, *Jesus Christ in the Old Testament*, London, 1965.

6. Irenaeus of Lyon, in the second century, no less than the author of Acts, regarded the existence of this body of Old Testament texts as proof of the truth of Christianity and the historicity of the Passion narratives. He tells the story, and at the same time adduces the testimonies: "Some . . . saw him weak and without glory, knowing how to bear weakness (Isa. 53:2), and seated upon the foal of an ass to come to Jerusalem (Zech. 9:9) giving his back to the whips, and his cheeks to the blows of men's hands (Isa. 50:6); led like a sheep to the slaughter (Isa. 53:7), given gall and vinegar to drink (Ps. 68:22); abandoned by his friends and kinsmen (Ps. 37:12), stretching out his hands all the day (Isa. 65:2), mocked and cursed by those who watched him (Ps. 21:7–9), his clothes divided, and lots cast for his garments (Ps. 21:19)." (*Adversus Haereses*, IV. 33.12, quoted by J. Daniélou, *History of Early Christian Doctrine*, translated by J. A. Baker, London, 1973, II, 231.)

7. Daniélou II, 215. Daniélou calls this an instance of "that christologizing of the O.T. *testimonia* which is a characteristic trait of Judaeo-Christianity." I have heard this example contested on the ground that we cannot be sure there were not Septuagint manuscripts that included the words *apo tou xulou* ("from the tree"). An explanation of how such an intrusive reading might have come about is this: a translator, coming across the Hebrew word *selah*, which, though it is not infrequent in the Psalms, has no certain meaning, transliterated it into Greek *xela* or even *xyla*, so that the text read "The Lord shall reign *xyla*." The addition was modified to *xylou*, and somebody then made sense of it by inserting *apo* and reading *apo xulou*, "from the

tree" — thus "manufacturing a prophecy of the crucifixion which was to be welcomed by Christian exegetes" (R. P. C. Hanson in *CHB*, I, 421).

8. Daniélou, II, 211.

9. Modern commentators sometimes propose testimonies, and there is of course no way of knowing whether these recently noticed relationships were in the minds of the writers. One instance would be the texts in Genesis and Amos supposed to have been used in Mark 14:51–52 (Chapter 3 above); another would be the derivation of the kiss of Judas from Proverbs 27:6 ("the kisses of an enemy are perfidious").

10. W. Maurer, *Kirche und Synagoge*, quoted in Von Campenhausen, *Formation of the Christian Bible*, p. 70, n. 57.

11. Thomas Pynchon, *The Crying of Lot 49*, New York, 1966, pp. 50–51.

12. This expression derives from an essay of Roland Barthes, "L'Effet du réel," *Communications*, 11 (1968): 84–89.

13. Martin Dibelius, quoted in D. E. Nineham, *The Gospel of St. Mark*, Harmondsworth, 1963, p. 421.

14. C. H. Dodd, *Historical Tradition in the Fourth Gospel*, Cambridge, 1963, pp. 31f.

15. Dodd, pp. 47f. Further defenses of the historicity of the events alluded to are offered by Pierre Benoit, *Jesus and the Gospel*, I, translated by Benet Weatherhead, London, 1973 (a Catholic work).

16. For an attempt to reconcile the accounts, see Benoit, pp. 123f.

17. Jeremias, *The Eucharistic Words of Jesus*, pp. 78–79, argues, that the charge was of false prophecy and that execution for this crime was required to be carried out at a feast "before all the people."

18. The conjecture of Paul Winter, *On the Trial of Jesus*, pp. 142f. He further suggests that the story as we have it arose out of there being two prisoners called Jesus (the "thief" is called "Jesus Bar-Abbas" in some witnesses) and from Pilate's having to find out which was the right one to try.

19. See, for example, S. G. F. Brandon, *Jesus and the Zealots*, Manchester, 1967, and *The Trial of Jesus*, London, 1968.

20. Quoted in W. Horbury, "The Trial of Jesus in Jewish Tradition," in *The Trial of Jesus*, ed. Ernst Bammel, Studies in Biblical Theology, second series, 13, London, 1970, p. 113.

21. See *The Times Literary Supplement*, 19 August 1977, p. 998.

22. The term is Gerard Genette's; his fuller classification would perhaps be "heterodiegetic internal analepsis," but it is interesting that none of his options seems to be a perfect fit in this case. See his

Figures III, Paris, 1972, and Shlomith Rimmon, "A Comprehensive Theory of Narrative," *PTL: a Journal for Descriptive Poetics and Theory of Literature*, I (1976): 33–62.

23. John Searle, "The Logical Status of Fictional Discourse," *New Literary History*, 6 (1974/5): 319–332.

24. Jean Starobinski, "Le Démoniaque de Gérasa: analyse littéraire de Marc 5:1–20," in R. Barthes and others, *Analyse structurale et exégèse biblique*, Paris, 1971, pp. 63–94; and in *Trois fureurs* ("Le Combat avec Légion"), Paris, 1974, 73–126. English translation in *New Literary History*, 4 (1973): 331–356.

25. Roland Barthes, "Le discours de l'histoire," *Social Science Information*, 6.4 (1967): 65–75.

26. Perhaps one should note here the assumption of modern semiologists that the "meaning" of a sign-vehicle never has a corresponding object (see Umberto Eco, *Theory of Semiotics*, Bloomington, 1976, pp. 58f). The social conventions governing the use of language are such that it has practical consequences: in Eco's example, if I tell you your house is on fire you will probably hurry home; but it may or may not be burning. More pointedly, the sentence "Napoleon died at Saint Helena on May 5, 1821" does not, for the semiologist, constitute something that is historically true, but merely shows that there exist in our culture codes such that sentences of this kind connote "historical truth."

27. W. B. Gallie, *Philosophy and Historical Understanding*, New York, 1964. John Drury, privately, makes the interesting point that Luke in his preface (1:1) announces that his plan is to set out his narrative sequentially (*kathexēs*), or in other words to give the story followability.

28. Arthur Danto, *Analytic Philosophy of History*, New York, 1965, p. 132.

29. Gallie, p. 64.

30. White, *Foundations of Historical Knowledge*, p. 222.

31. Quoted in Morton White, p. 261.

32. *Knowledge and Human Interests*, p. 273.

33. See note 24.

34. *Works of Spinoza*, translated by R. H. M. Elwes, London, 1883, I, 101f.

35. Hans Frei, *The Eclipse of Biblical Narrative*, New Haven, 1974, p. 41.

36. Frei, p. 187.

37. Frei, pp. 142f. Frei has an interesting quotation from a letter

of Richardson's, in which the novelist explains that he wishes to maintain the fiction that Clarissa's letters were real, not because he wished them to be "*thought* genuine," but, among other reasons, in order "to avoid hurting that kind of Historical Faith which Fiction itself is genuinely read with, tho' we know it to be Fiction" (p. 144). For a useful study of the relations of fact and fiction in literary theory before, during, and after the Renaissance, see W. B. Nelson, *Fact and Fiction: The Dilemma of the Renaissance Storyteller*, Cambridge, Mass., 1973.

38. J. Hillis Miller, "Narrative and History," *ELH*, 41 (1974): 455–473.

VI. The Unfollowable World

1. Augustine, *Sermons on the New Testament*, Oxford, 1854, I, 377ff.

2. Howard C. Kee, *Community of the New Age*, London, 1977, p. 54, lists eight, but omits the case of the strange exorcist (9:38–41) and more understandably does not treat the whole of Chapter 13 as an intercalation.

3. See Taylor, *St. Mark*, pp. 191–192 (citing Bultmann and others).

4. Kee, p. 56.

5. Kee, p. 55.

6. Erich Auerbach, *Mimesis*, Princeton, 1953, Chap. I. It should be said that the argument seems to have little appeal to hellenists.

7. There were, later, differences between the followers of John and those of Jesus; the Marcan account exploits certain parallels, but always emphasizes the preparatory role of John.

8. Taylor, *St. Mark*, p. 307, Drury, *Tradition and Design*, p. 95, Nineham, *Mark*, p. 172.

9. Kee, *Community of the New Age*, p. 55.

10. The presumably authentic account of John in Josephus (*Ant.* xviii.5.2) suggests that Herod arrested and executed John because of his power to inflame the people; he wished to prevent riots. The story of the promise to Salome, grafted on to this historical detail, probably derives from Esther 5:3, where the king over his wine says he will give Esther what she asks, up to half of his kingdom. For Mark's use of the same passage in the story of the daughter of Jairus, see below.

11. Taylor, *St. Mark*, p. 289.

12. Q. Quesnell, *The Mind of Mark*, Analecta Biblica, Rome, 1969, p. 38, sees this as part of a very elaborate bread symbolism in Mark.

13. Taylor, p. 227.
14. Cranfield, *St. Mark*, p. 179.
15. See Chapter Five, note 24 above.
16. Kee, *Community of the New Age*, pp. 64f.
17. There is a useful survey of a good many outlines in Kee, Chap. III; see also the bibliographies in W. G. Kümmel, *Introduction to the New Testament*, translated by H. C. Kee, London, 1975, the commentary of Cranfield, Farrer's books cited above, and E. Trocmé, *The Formation of the Gospel according to Mark*, translated by Pamela Gaughan, London, 1975.
18. William Wrede, *The Messianic Secret in the Gospels*, translated by J. C. G. Greig, Greenwood, South Carolina, 1971.
19. This seems to be the meaning of *hoi par autou* in 3:21.
20. Discussions of the gospel as genre seem not to have benefited from the interest of secular critics in genre theory. What W. Marxsen says, that Mark instituted the genre of gospel, and thenceforth a gospel was the sort of thing Mark wrote ("after Mark I:1 the Gospels are called Gospels"; *Mark the Evangelist*, translated by J. Boyce, Nashville, 1969, p. 125), may be true but it is not helpful (the sense of the word in that place is much disputed; and there are considerable differences between the four gospels, John being particularly remote from Mark). Attempts to show that the genre derived from some existing type (the Hellenistic aretalogy, the Jewish *beracah*, eschatological prophecy) do not survive scrutiny; as Amos Wilder puts it, gospel was "the only wholly new *genre* created by the Church, and the author of Mark receives the credit for it" (*Early Christian Rhetoric*, second ed., Cambridge, Mass., 1971, p. 28). Kee surveys the various attempts to find the paradigm of gospel in existing genres (*Community of the New Age*, pp. 17–30) and agrees with Wilder. Yet the statement that Mark founded a new genre does not entail that it is unrelated to all others. If it had been so it would have been practically unreadable. A genre is not what used to be known as a *kind*, with rules prescribed by institutional authority; it is a context of expectation, an "internalized probability system" (Leonard Meyer, *Music, the Arts and Ideas*, Chicago, 1967). It is the equivalent, for a longer discourse, of the set of expectations which enables us to follow a sentence as it is spoken. Only if the set of these expectations has been extrapolated into a body of rules (as when the institution made kinds prescriptive) will it become sensible to argue as to whether John is or is not a gospel.

New genres are formed from realignments of existing genres. To prove that a gospel is evidently not a *chria* or an aretalogy or a *beracah* or an apocalypse is by no means to demonstrate that these genres did not contribute to the set of expectations within which Mark wrote and his audience read or listened. The forms of attention required will have been established by other genres; thus the people who had difficulty with Ariosto's *Orlando Furioso* were the learned, who quarreled about its being epic or romance. What it called for, and got from the lay reader, was a new kind of attention related to several existing genres (see C. Guillén, *Literature as System*, Princeton, 1971, pp. 121f). The new game is not identical with the others; but if there had been no others we should not be able to play. As Frederic Jameson puts it, a shade too strongly perhaps, for he is a Marxist, "the historical moment blocks off a certain number of formal possibilities which had been available in former situations, all the while opening up determinate new ones" ("Magical Narratives: Romance as Genre," *New Literary History*, 7 (1975/6): 135–163). Historically, like any new form of literature, the gospel is *genus mixtum*, just like *Orlando Furioso* and *Il Pastor Fido*, though there was no academy to be thrown into confusion by Mark's mixtures. On these matters see also E. D. Hirsch, Jr., *Validity in Interpretation*, New Haven, 1967, and *The Aims of Interpretation*, Chicago, 1976.

If genre is a consensus, a set of fore-understandings exterior to a text which enable us to follow that text, whether it is a sentence, a book, or a life, its existence explains why readers who share those fore-understandings rather exactly with the author of the text can read him more easily; but it also explains why we must read him differently. The generic assumptions common to Mark and his readers are forgotten, and scholarship at best recovers a faint image of them. They have descendants, but the family likeness is dilute. That is why the kind of openness to interpretation insisted upon by Starobinski, and by me, is not an act of defiance but an inevitable historical fact. It is equally inevitable, granted the enormous cultural importance of the gospels over so long a period, that we inherit other fore-understandings, many of them none the less arbitrary for being so rarely called into question; these are the forces that limit the possible senses of the work under consideration.

21. Hans von Campenhausen, *The Formation of the Christian Bible*, p. 300. How early the practice of deliberate concealment affected the gospels is uncertain; but it is sometimes cited as the reason why Mark ends where he does, and why, unlike Matthew and Luke, he says little about the temptation in the wilderness (J. Jeremias, *Eucharistic Words*, p. 132).

Index

120
81 f.
137
58-60
60-64